Beyond the Far Ridge

M000188784

Other books by Edward Mark McGough:

Young Rider of the High Country
Young Rider Meets a Challenge
Young Rider on the Twisting Trail

Beyond the Far Ridge

Pioneering in the
Rocky Mountain High Country

by
Edward Mark McGough

illustrations by Victoria Bales

HIGH PLAINS PRESS

The text of this book is biographical in scope;
however, out of consideration for the
privacy of individuals involved,
personal names and place names have been changed.

LIBRARY OF CONGRESS CATALOGING-IN-PUBLICATION DATA
McGough, Edward Mark
    Beyond the far ridge : pioneering in the Rocky Mountain high
country / by Edward Mark McGough; illustrations by Victoria Bales.
        p. cm.
ISBN 0-931271-15-0
        1. Mountain life—Wyoming. 2. Mountain life—Rocky Mountains.
3. Wyoming—Social life and customs. 4. McGough, Edward Mark,
1917- —Homes and haunts—Wyoming. I. Title.
F761.M37   1991   91-32596
978.7'00943—dc20   CIP

Copyright © 1992 Edward Mark McGough
All Rights Reserved.
Printed in the United States of America.

HIGH PLAINS PRESS
Glendo, Wyoming 82213

CONTENTS

To all those people who had a dream
but never got to live
"beyond the far ridge."

Introduction

HAVE YOU EVER thought of living in some remote place, far beyond the end of tire tracks? Maybe you've thought of a country where you could make your way to some high, rockbound rim and look over a vast sweep of mountain ranges where tall snow-capped peaks reach for blue sky. In your mind's eye, perhaps you saw long, grassy parks showing up like emerald islands in a darker green sea of pine and spruce. And have you ever dreamed of peering into some dark canyon, where a white water stream plunges and splashes over granite boulders in a violent rush toward lower country?

Mary and I thought about a country like that for over thirty years. Finally, there came a day when we pulled stakes, loaded our outfit on a string of pack horses, and headed up the mountain. At eight thousand feet, we pitched our tent. Working all through the winter, we built a cabin. It became our home, summer and winter.

Our neighbors were the animal dwellers of the high country. Usually, it was May or June before we got to enjoy our Christmas mail. In the winter, Mary and I explored the mountain on snowshoes. During the grazing season, we herded cattle on horseback.

If you've got the time to listen for a spell, pull up a chair, and we'll share our unique adventure.

E. M. M.

Up to the High Country

S OME YEARS BACK on a bright day in early June, Mary and I rode our horses up the mountain to start a high country venture that changed our lives forever.

I recall the day in detail. The sun, bearing down between scattered cumulus clouds, promised grass-growing heat well before noon. Buttercups and lupine splashed the open slopes with yellow and blue, as meadowlarks lent heart-lifting music to the morning. I remember those things because they came at a time when we were phasing out an important era in our lives and commencing another.

Mary and I reined in our horses at a view-point on the rough mountain trail. The climb along the side of Gunshot Canyon was a steep one. Even with grain-fed, hard-muscled horses, experience told us to go slow and to rest often.

We turned in our saddles and let our eyes sweep over as good a chunk of cow country as there is in the Rocky Mountain West, where foothills and meadows stretch out as a rolling carpet of lush green grass. Far below us, we could make out the red and white cluster of buildings that made up the headquarters of the family-owned cattle ranch for whom we had worked for many years.

Looking up the creek-bottom valley that led toward the upper foothills, we recognized pastures we knew by name, by size, and by shape. At length, our eyes focused on the rooftops of the homes and barns of the Deer Creek Place.

The Deer Creek Place was the home base for the Hereford purebred cow herd. We had lived there for a long time and considered it our home. The people who owned the ranch, of which the Deer Creek Place was a part, were not only our employers but our good friends, too. Our children grew up there, living the interesting life of typical ranch youngsters before they went their separate ways.

As Mary and I looked down on the Deer Creek Place that June day, we found it difficult to keep nostalgia from creeping in. We liked the big white house and thought of evenings in the cozy living room with its low-beamed ceiling and blazing fireplace. Often, I went to sleep there with a book on my chest.

Then we remembered the people, young and old, who had worked at the place through the years. They became our good friends, and their staunch support made my job easier.

I knew every cow in the herd by sight and by pedigree. I had tagged them as calves the day they were born and had followed their record of performance ever since.

I guess the small things made the Deer Creek Place special in our thoughts that day. Whenever Mary crossed the bridge to get our mail on the county road, she stopped for awhile to visit with her friend, the dipper. That water-loving bird bobbed up and down on a rock in mid-stream, then walked beneath the surface in search of bugs for lunch.

The ranch shop had been constructed of logs many years ago, and that age gave it character of a sort. On its walls hung ancient pieces of handcrafted hardware made by a blacksmith of an earlier time. The stuff wasn't used. It might never be used. But it was part of the place.

As we looked down on the Deer Creek, Mary mentioned the wild turkeys who had occasionally paraded through the yard, and in the winter, the deer who ate chaff off the bed of the hay sled parked near the barn.

I recalled the teams of stout draft horses who, at different times, pulled that sled across the meadows as we fed hay to the cattle. Our first team was the Clydesdales, Jack and Jerry. Then came the Belgians, Duke and Dandy, and later, another young team of Belgians whom Mary named Nip and Tuck.

On those mornings, from my place on the sled, I liked to look down on those broad backs and feel the power of the horses come to me through the long leather lines I held in my hands. Best of all, I liked to be greeted by a friendly nicker when the back door slammed as I headed for the barn in the morning.

ø ø ø

From under my left stirrup, Skipper, our Dingo cow dog, looked up and whined impatiently, as if to tell us we had looked back long enough. He was right. It was time to look up and ahead.

ø ø ø

Mary and I always meet each new day as another adventure in the making. They all seem to present a challenge of some sort.

As we reined our horses around and continued up the trail, I was reminded that the new life we were heading into would cause us to face a completely new set of challenges. Before the sun set that night, we would be camped on the privately-owned, high country, summer range of the ranch. In that primitive setting, we would live and work. The first thing we needed to accomplish was building a house of logs. That done, and as time went along, I would take on the job of caring for whatever cattle the ranch pastured up there on our end of the mountain. I also planned to ride for a cattle association that runs stock, on a fee basis, on adjacent rented pasture.

I looked back over my shoulder. Mary met my eyes and smiled without speaking. With a woman like that at my side, let the challenges come as they may.

ø ø ø

That day we led four pack horses loaded down with food, tools, and bedrolls. I had been making trips up the mountain whenever I could get away from Deer Creek, so we already had supplies cached away on top.

I led Bridger, the number one horse in the string. Bridger was a big, stout horse, as gentle and sensible as they come. But that morning, he rolled his eyes and snorted through his nose, acting like a bronc that had never been packed before. He gave every indication that he had no liking for the live cargo riding atop his load.

Tiger Lily was our favorite cat down at Deer Creek. She was the only really gentle cat among all the barn cats on the place. Mary and I had talked it over. Surely if we established a new home on the mountain, Tiger Lily had to come along as we moved. Right then, she was telling us she would rather be back at the barn.

We had borrowed a cat travel cage from some friends. It was a rather fancy thing made out of varnished plywood with little round holes along the side so a cat could get air. We set it atop Bridger's load and snugged it down under the diamond hitch. As the horse clawed his way up the steep mountain trail, the cage jerked back and forth and swayed from side to side. Probably not a comfortable ride for a cat.

From inside the cage, Tiger Lily made it clear she was unhappy. She scratched and howled and caterwauled worse than any she-cat and he-cat making whoopee under a bedroom window. And every time Tiger Lily carried on like that, Skipper trotted up from his place at the heels of the last pack horse. At Bridger's side, the dog looked up and cocked his head. He couldn't see the cat, but he sure knew cat noises.

By then, Bridger had more sweat showing than even that steep trail should have brought out. Every time the cat made those weird noises, he tucked his tail between his legs and scooted ahead until his chin rested on my knee.

But steep mountain trails, if they are long enough, have a way of making skittish horses quiet. As time went on, Bridger just looked back over his shoulder at the cat cage instead of charging ahead. By the time we pulled into camp, I think we could have tossed a mountain lion on the horse, and he wouldn't have cared much.

ø ø ø

One evening about three weeks later, Mary and I sat out in front of our tent. We just took our ease and talked about the things we had accomplished so far and about the things we hoped to get done as time went on.

Down the grassy slope, we heard the horse bell making mountain music in the early twilight. Except for a wrangle horse we kept in close, we had turned the string loose to graze at will. They were all horses that had been running together at Deer Creek, so they would stay in a bunch. We had put a bell on one horse to help us locate them whenever they wandered out of sight.

Over toward the west, we saw a mule deer doe and her fawn move out of the timber. With dainty steps, they made their way to a patch of clover. The doe nibbled on the tender leaves while her fawn sniffed at larkspur blossoms and looked around.

Close at hand, but out of sight, robins let the world know they were well and happy.

ø ø ø

I've always said Mary could make a home atop a fence post. With the tent to work with, she had a running start. Already we had a home.

In a ten-by-twelve-foot tent with four-foot walls, we didn't have much room for furniture. We cut down to the basics.

We built a double bed at the back end of the tent. Near the front end, we set up a Sims stove which is pretty much like the standard sheepherder's stove, only it can be folded for easier packing on a horse. To make it more convenient to cook on, I built a wooden stand to elevate it to conventional stove height.

We used two canvas folding chairs. For a table at mealtime, we placed a piece of plywood on the bed. In the evening, the same piece of plywood served as a writing desk when it was propped on one's knees.

We lined up two plywood kitchen panniers along the west wall. They were the kind carried on a pack horse, and they served as our kitchen cabinets. A couple of army steel ammunition boxes came in handy for general kitchen storage and were rodent-proof. Near the stove we placed a stack of split wood. Finally, I made a low platform to hold our covered water bucket.

Outside, between two trees, I built a wash bench to hold our enamel wash basin and soap dish. Nails driven into a tree held our toothbrushes and a small mirror. I strung a clothesline overhead, between the two trees. That held our towels. Our wash-up place was only a few steps from the tent, so it was easy to get warm water.

ø ø ø

We had no sooner settled into our home under canvas when winter returned to the high country. About two in the morning we woke up to find snow blowing in under the flaps. At daylight it was still snowing with about six inches already on the ground. The snowfall continued all day—big, white, sticky flakes heavily laden with moisture. By evening, a foot and a half of snow had built up. Just before dark our horses drifted by, and I gave them a handout of grain cake. They then moved on to the shelter of a thick stand of pine.

With reluctance, Tiger Lily went outside to answer a call of nature. She didn't waste much time. Bounding through the deep snow, she broke the track record getting back to the tent. Inside, she jumped up on a stack of wood near the stove and got busy drying herself off.

Skipper was made of stauncher stuff. He struggled a full fifty yards through the wet snow, barked a few times at nothing particular, then followed his own trail back to the tent.

When we peeked out of our tent early the next morning, the sky was clear. All around us the boughs of the pines, spruces, and firs were weighed down by the heavy snow. By the time the sun added its bright light to the scene, the entire mountainside looked like a Christmas card of the nicest kind.

Late snowstorms have a way of striking with sudden vengeance, and they leave their mark on the land. But when the heat of the sun bears down on the moisture-heavy snow, it settles in an amazingly short time. Soon, the snow lingers only in the timber. The grassy slopes bare off, and most of the wildflowers lift their nodding heads. Again the welcome signs of early summer return to the high country.

ø ø ø

Up the slope, behind the tent a short way, a never-failing spring of fresh mountain water bubbled up through clean, sparkling gravel. Nothing had been done to the spring by way of development. For the time being, I figured nothing was necessary. Mary changed my mind about that. It seems she found our dog taking a bath there one warm afternoon

All other work came to a halt while I built a covered spring box from some redwood lumber I had packed in earlier.

While I was at it, I constructed another covered box that I set in beside the spring box. We called it our refrigerator. It was a handy place to keep perishable food from spoiling. I filled in all around both boxes with small rocks and gravel. They were well anchored, and the gravel provided a clean, dry place for us to walk on whenever we went to the spring.

Soon the cattle would be moved up to summer range, so we needed a fence around our camp. Cows have been known to be inquisitive neighbors. The fence would serve another purpose. We planned the enclosure to be big enough to make a handy night pasture for horses when needed.

A buck fence of peeled poles would have been more to our liking, but, for the sake of expediency, we used barbed wire. But our gates, four in number, we built of peeled poles. A pole gate is handy, and we think they look good.

By now, the place was beginning to look like the start of a cow camp. But truly, for the touch of permanence we needed a cabin. A cabin born of the high country. A cabin built of logs and some native stone.

Skidding Logs

WE HAD TO GO up the hill, north of our camp, to cut house logs. There the lodgepole pine grew tall and with very little taper. We were fortunate to have dry timber to select from—both standing dead trees and windfalls lying crisscross above the ground. Nature has ways of thinning out stands of timber. Sometimes it works to a man's advantage.

Through the years, I had spent more time chasing cows than operating a chain saw. There was a lot about logging I didn't know. But, if Mary and I were going to accomplish what we had in mind, I had to learn fast.

Luckily, we had a friend who ran a post and pole operation, as well as a small ranch. Carson is an expert at handling a chain saw and, in addition, is a good hand at skidding with a horse. Carson spent a day with me, and the pointers he gave me were a big help.

I well remember the first trees I felled. I looked up the trunk of one of those lodgepoles and thought it reached halfway to the sky. Then I tried to figure out how I could make it land where I wanted it to when it fell. By the time I started the chain saw and bent over to make my cut, I had a feeling in my stomach like I get when I think a horse is going to buck with me.

But time and experience cure many things. Each day I

started out early in the morning when the air was cool and I was fresh. Sometimes, I had no trouble finding house-log trees to my liking. Then again, sometimes I looked and looked for what I wanted. It seemed the trees were either too big or too small, or they were not straight enough. Or some had spiral cracks.

Fatigue was something I hadn't thought much about. But I found that manhandling one of those big sticks to the edge of the skid trail caused a man to want to bed down soon after supper. Actually, it was a case of lack of experience and using a new set of muscles. As time went on, I toughened to the job and learned how to work in the timber.

A lot of accidents happen working in the timber. I didn't want to become another statistic, and Mary didn't want me to become one either. She came up late in the morning and watched me work. If she noticed my reflexes slowing down, she suggested I quit logging for awhile. It wasn't hard for me to find something else to work at, and all of it pertained to building a house out of logs.

For instance, rock foundation piers needed to be set up before the sill logs could be laid. On a ridge, less than a quarter mile from our building site, we had a good source of red rock. It was just the thing for building piers, as I could easily find rocks with two flat opposite sides.

I had already built a stone boat—a flat sledge without runners—to move the rock to camp. We had brought up Nip, a four-year old Belgian gelding. He was one-half of the feed team of Nip and Tuck used at Deer Creek. We now gave him a new job.

Nip had never worked alone. After I hooked him up to the stone boat, we made some pretty fast circles around a small meadow before he settled down enough for me to haul rock. I still had to take big, long strides all afternoon to keep up with the horse. Anyhow, we managed to haul five loads before supper.

As one day moved into the next, my skid trails reached back like the branches of a tree. Along the cleared trails, I stockpiled logs ready to be moved down to our building site. The lengths ranged from eighteen to twenty-four feet. I pointed the butt ends of the  logs, mostly eight inches in diameter, toward camp. I stacked them across whatever handy pole or small log I could find.

Finally, one morning when the sun was not up yet, I got Nip in. I grained him before breakfast and went to eat my own. This was the day I was to start skidding. I was a bit apprehensive. My previous experience along this line had been dragging in firewood from atop a saddle horse.

After breakfast I harnessed Nip and hooked him up to the skid sled, the toboggan-like implement on which I would secure the butt ends of the logs for moving. Nip moved off, his head down, his chin tucked in. That young Belgian always started the same, loaded or empty, like he was ready to move a mountain if you asked him to. There was no slack in the lines as I made hurry-up steps to keep up.

At the foot of the steep trail leading up to the logging area, I rested a moment. The trail looked longer and more treacherous than it did the day before. In a short while, I would be coming down that chute with the first load of logs.

Nip stepped nervously in place. I let him move on. Looking at his broad, heavily muscled hindquarters, I thought of the first time I had seen the sorrel horse.

Mary and I had gone back to the Waverly Draft Horse

Sale in Iowa. Our errand was to buy a young team for the ranch, to be used at Deer Creek. Looking over three hundred fifty young, well-groomed horses was enough to boggle the mind. We looked for a day and a half and changed our minds a half-dozen times.

We went back several times to the stall of a team from Minnesota. They were big, flat-boned colts, and they looked like they would grow some more. Late in the day of the sale, we bid on the pair. Our bid was highest. We had bought the young team. On the way home, they became Nip and Tuck.

At Deer Creek, Wes was our teamster. He had gentle hands and was good with young horses. Wes brought the colts along nicely, working them light the first winter and harder as they became four years old.

Now as we topped out at the head of the steep trail, I was puffing hard. I looked at Nip's flanks. The climb hadn't fazed him. After we got on top, the trail followed an easy grade to the logging area.

There I turned Nip around and stopped the skid sled handy to a pile of logs along the trail. I unhooked the tugs, which hitched the horse to the sled, and tossed them aside, so the horse couldn't step on them. Nip was good at standing, but just in case he did take off, he couldn't drag anything behind him. I folded the lines across his rump and started to load.

The skid sled measured about three feet long. At the front end, a heavy bar, raised six inches above the boiler plate floor of the sled, made a platform to receive the butt end of the logs. I loaded three logs and chained each separately with a timberman's hitch. Over the three, I passed another light chain and boomed it snug with a chain tightener.

Then wiping some sweat out of my eyes with a shirt sleeve, I pulled up my gloves until they were snug. When I gathered up the lines, Nip turned his head and watched as I hooked up the tug chains. I straightened out those long leather lines so I wouldn't get my feet tangled and looked ahead at the route I would take. I had a straight shot for twenty-five yards.

Speaking quietly to Nip, I eased him forward into the collar. The horse shifted his front end from side to side, waiting. I tightened my grip on the lines and gave Nip his cue. The big sorrel leaned forward; the tugs tightened. He lowered his head and dug his feet into the soft earth. The horse moved ahead, and behind him the load of lodgepole pine moved, too.

Three logs were no chore for a horse that had pulled a loaded hay sled all the winter through. Nip liked to pull. I remember, when Nip was a colt, Wes used to say, "He's all work." If Nip had a fault, it was that he wanted to work too fast. Besides, he had been loafing on good pasture since the end of calving season. The gelding had a lot of stored-up energy to use. I lay back on the lines, but I was pulled along in stiff-legged, bounding strides.

Behind Nip and me, the logs bounced over rocks, bumping together and rumbling like distant thunder. Dry limbs in the way were snapped and tossed aside.

Soon the trail bent to the left on a slight upgrade. Nip responded to direction nicely. A big rock came up on the right. I swung the horse wide to miss it; even so, the load scraped hard.

Ahead the trail led between two trees. Yesterday that passage seemed wide, with room to spare. As we came up fast now, it looked dangerously narrow for horse and man and load. I had heard of men breaking a leg, caught between skidding logs and standing trees.

I walked the lines until I was alongside the sled at the head of the rumbling load. Nip jerked his head and flicked his ears, as though measuring the space ahead. We made our

Victoria 1990

entry head-on. I shifted my hips toward the sled and tucked in an elbow. We slipped through without scraping a log.

And so it went until we reached the top of the steep hill. I pulled up the horse. Nip didn't look as though he needed a rest, but I sure wanted to take a breather. Never letting loose of the lines, I retightened the chain across the load.

When I straightened up, I looked along Nip's long body at the trail down which I had to travel in a moment. The trail looked steeper, and longer, and more sidling than ever. In places huge rocks encroached on the trail, narrowing the passage to the slimmest track.

I moved over to the uphill side of the load and gathered up the slack in the lines. When I gave Nip a vocal command, he started down. It was easier for the horse to move the load on the downgrade, so he slowed his pace a bit. The sharp sidefall of the land gave me a problem. It was hard to keep the skid sled on the trail. I had to keep Nip climbing the bank on the uphill side of the trail, stepping sideways to hold the head of the load in place.

Bounding over rocks like a mountain goat, I used my eyes to search for safe passage for my feet. This was no time to stumble and fall and maybe lose my grip on the lines. I watched the direction Nip's head took and the aim of the front of the sled. I never turned to look at the logs. Where the head went, the tail had to follow.

When we got to the bottom, I breathed easier. It hadn't been so bad after all. Neither man nor beast had been hurt, and we never lost a log. Soon we pulled up at the place where I was to stockpile the logs. I unhooked the tugs and tossed the lines over Nip's back. Walking forward, I patted the horse on his deep, thick neck.

And so it went for many days. Nip improved as a skid horse as time moved along. He worked more slowly and learned how to handle himself on every twist and turn of the trail. As for myself, I really got legged-up on that job. I used to say there wasn't an elk on the mountain that could get away from me.

During those days, Nip was guilty of only one infraction that tainted his reputation.

One night it snowed. Not much, but enough so that Mary scraped some off the roof of the tent and packed it down into a water bucket. She thought snow water would be just the thing in which to wash her hair. Mary didn't get around to the job as soon as she planned. The bucket of snow water rested on the wash bench for a couple of days.

I came in one noon with Nip. I grained him, pulled off his harness, and turned him loose. The horse rolled in the green grass, then ambled up toward the tent. The next sound I heard was Mary on the warpath after Nip. Our skid horse had a nice little creek handy for drinking. But he preferred Mary's hair wash water instead. A few loud gulps, and Nip had drained the bucket.

After awhile, Mary laughed. She considered it a good trade. All those logs for a bucket of snow water.

 Building with Logs

I LIKE TO PEEL logs. That is, if I have a good sharp drawknife. Well, I had a good sharp drawknife which was close to a hundred years old. The tool had the look of iron shaped by the hand of a master craftsman. As I sat on a log carefully working an oil stone along the knife's well-worn blade, I felt I had a legacy of a sort in my hands. A legacy to respect and to use as my father had before me.

One of the nice things about peeling logs is that you get a quick return on your investment of energy. Each time you draw that sharp blade to you, a slice of brown, scaly bark falls to the ground. In its place, new wood shows clean and smooth. Putting a log up on sawhorses brings it to a convenient height. All a man has to do is walk along and make sure the drawknife does its job.

As you peel along and admire your work, you can learn something of tree history, too. Under the bark you might find some logs are stained blue. It tells you pine beetles have brought the spores of bluestain fungi into the tree. These sprout and clog the tree's water-conducting system. The tree weakens and dies of thirst. Here and there, pock marks show where a woodpecker searched for eggs and larvae of the invading beetle.

By now you have warmed up a bit, and your arms need a short rest. You walk to the butt end of the log and count the rings of annual growth. In the early life of the tree, the rings were well-spaced. You know its roots took in good moisture those years. You count along, and the distance between the rings is closer. Those were the years when water was scarce.

You begin your count again because you lost track as you thought of tree history instead of the tally. Fifty annual rings it is. Fifty years of tree life. A youngster compared with some of the Douglas fir and Engelmann spruce on the mountain. You chuckle. The tree was a seedling when you thought you were almost a man. You think again. There is a span of tree history you know little about. How long did the tree stand as a lifeless skeleton in the living forest?

ø ø ø

Mary and I peeled many logs together; she at one end, me at the other. As we worked along, we talked and laughed. Mary said she liked to peel logs because the job built up her muscles. Then she could load a pack horse easier. An image formed in my mind's eye. I wondered what it would be like to be married to a muscle-bound woman weighing a hundred and ten pounds.

ø ø ø

During this time, we had visitors off and on—neighbors who trailed cattle to the mountains. After they turned their herd loose on their allotted area, they stopped by and paid their respects. We were complimented by their interest and grateful for their moral support.

Next to our camp came the bovine sidewalk engineers. Promptly at nine they came on schedule, day after day, as though they were bossing a big construction job in town. Two-year-old heifers with their first calves are in a personality class of their own. They haven't quite thrown off all the traits of yearlings. Nor, try as they may, have they acquired all the mature dignity of cows.

Each day they lined up along the fence, shoving and pushing to get the best place. There they stood for an hour or more, chewing their cuds, watching our job go on.

ø ø ø

It was an important day for us when we finally set the sill logs on the foundation piers. We selected the biggest, straightest, and soundest logs from our pile of peeled logs to use as sills. We cut saddle notches in the first cross logs and set them in place on the sills.

We spiked floor joists on twenty-four-inch centers along the sills and laid the subfloor. Each time we started a new course of logs in the wall, we reversed the butt ends in order to keep the top line level. Wall logs averaged eight inches at the butt end.

I found that building with logs did not go as fast as I planned. I proved to be especially slow at fitting saddle notches. Mary said I was trying to fit logs like a cabinet maker. One evening, just before supper, she threatened to quit if I tried to make a certain notch fit closer.

The summer moved along faster than I wanted. At the end of each day I measured from floor to the top of the last log laid. It seemed it was taking too long for the walls to reach the height where the important plate log could be rolled into place. Nevertheless, when I walked up the hill toward the tent, I always stopped and turned to evaluate my work from a distance. It was then I was encouraged to go on. I saw that each log laid really did make the project look more like a house in the making.

ø ø ø

Each day we saw more signs that fall was moving in on the high country. The range grass turned brown; more often we had frost in the morning and, sometimes, even a skiff of snow. Lupine was in the pod stage, but a few hardy asters and bluebells lent color to the landscape. Whenever we had rain and the sun warmed up the soil, dandelions came back for a colorful encore.

When our cattlemen friends stopped by for a visit, the talk turned to things like the weaning weight of calves. And how long before a change of weather would force ranchers to gather up and trail herds to the low country. Fall talk, it might be called.

Mary and I decided we would winter on the mountain. It meant we would discontinue building with logs for awhile and turn our heads and hands to other things.

We had some ideas about winterizing our tent to make a comfortable camp. We would need to skid in more logs for firewood. And we'd have to purchase and truck supplies of all kinds back to the Deer Creek Place.

There we would load our pack horses and start out for the mountain. The number of trips would be many. But we would take them one at a time, with a rest in between for the horses.

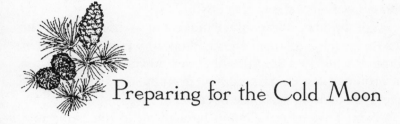 Preparing for the Cold Moon

ALTOGETHER, IT TURNED out to be a busy fall, although getting in firewood didn't take as much time as I thought it would. Looking for firewood wasn't like searching for dry trees to make house logs. I took wood as I found it without being concerned if it was straight or crooked, big or small, or if it had many cracks. With Nip's help, we soon had a pile of firewood logs that we figured would take us through the winter and well into the summer.

Getting in our winter supplies was another matter. At first the chore seemed staggering. Mary had the biggest job, estimating just how much foodstuff we'd require to carry us to green grass.

Mary stayed in town so she could strike out every morning to purchase supplies and get them out to the Deer Creek Place. An outbuilding there served us well both as a saddle room and as a storage place. Mary left stuff there for me to pick up later.

I made trips down off the mountain with three pack horses. As soon as I got to Deer Creek, I watered and grained the horses and then turned them loose with saddles on. They picked around on the grass close by.

In the storeroom, I saw what Mary had left for me. She'd packaged the supplies in boxes of a size and shape that would fit into our canvas panniers or would stack on our cargo carriers. She'd labeled each box with its contents and also with the weight of the loaded box.

For the steep climb up the mountain, we tried to hold our pack horse loads to about one hundred forty pounds. With that in mind, I lined up six piles of boxes down the center of the storeroom, each containing seventy pounds. I would pack seventy pounds on each side of each horse.

Next I went outside and latched on to the horse that would be number one in the string. I tied him to the hitch rail in front of the storeroom and started loading. Our horses are gentle. They have been packed often, so they hardly ever move a step.

As soon as I'd loaded the cargo, I tossed a tarp over the top. A double diamond hitch secured the entire load. Then I led the first horse to the corral fence nearby and tied him to a post.

So it went until three horses were packed. Then I hitched the strong halter rope of the second horse to the lighter weight breakaway rope tied to the pack saddle of number one horse. I tied the number three horse to number two in the same way.

Why do packers use a breakaway rope? Even with the best of well-mannered pack horses, accidents have been known to occur—and for any one of many reasons. For instance, scratching up a narrow, icy trail along the side of a deep canyon with a sheer drop off at the outer edge, a horse might have his front feet go out from under him and down he falls. When the lightweight breakaway rope receives the sudden stress, it breaks. With that connection removed, the horse that went down won't pull the rest of the string off their feet, and the chance of a serious accident is minimized.

When all was ready, I mounted with the lead rope of my number one pack horse in my hand. I gave a vocal signal to the string, and we moved out, headed for the mountain. I've led four pack horses, and even five, but three horses behind the rider is a nice way to go, especially if the trails weave through timber.

To make the round trip between our camp and Deer Creek in one day, I had to saddle up by Coleman lantern in the morning. And I had better plan to unpack by the same kind of light that evening.

I had made a platform of poles to place our supplies on. Covered with a heavy tarp and lashed down, it made a pretty good temporary cache.

By now the cattle were long off the mountain. With luck, we had a winter supply of game meat hanging from a pole. Snow covered the ground all the time, and below zero temperatures were common at night. The ride across the flats in the foothills made a fellow realize that winter was asking fall to move over. I swapped my Stetson for a Scotch cap and started wearing the heavy shotgun chaps Zeke made for me years ago.

Every round trip made the pile of boxes at Deer Creek get smaller and the mound of stuff near the tent get bigger. Our camp acquired the look of a place where someone was going to spend the winter.

One night, I returned to camp and Tiger Lily wasn't there to greet me. The cat sometimes climbed about in those craggy places up the hill from the tent, looking for any prey she thought she could handle. I worried she might have fallen victim to a coyote or a great horned owl.

However, my concern was unfounded. On my next trip down to Deer Creek, Tiger Lily was there at the ranch to greet me. She rubbed against my leg and purred. Maybe she was trying to tell me of the perils of her trip off the mountain. And that she liked the mountain all right, but, after all, the horse barn had been her home for so many winters.

Her job in town completed, Mary returned to the mountain. Skipper and I were glad to have her back. Soon she made our tent seem more like a winter home than ever.

About that time, we got a lift in our packing chore that I hadn't planned on, but welcomed wholeheartedly. A couple of hands from Deer Creek came up toward the end of elk season looking for meat. They led three extra pack horses loaded with our stuff. The word got around. Rancher neighbors, with elk camps spotted here and there along the little creeks, lent a hand. Instead of leading a string of empty pack horses up the mountain, they came loaded with our winter supplies. I guess it is possible to live without friends, but it is so much nicer to have them.

One night after dark, we heard someone hail the camp. I walked down to the east gate. There was Chip, a young fellow from one of the hunting camps. He led a pack mule. In the dim light I saw Chip's teeth showing white in a big smile. He slipped a wire cage out from under the pack tarp, and I heard something call, "Meow." Chip handed me the cage. With a cheery goodbye, he stepped aboard his saddle mare and led the mule through the timber, headed for his camp.

I carried the cage into the tent. There, under the light of the lantern, I set it on the bed while Mary and Skipper gathered around. I opened the door to the cage, and a little black and white kitten with long hair walked out. She looked around; blinking her eyes, she said, "Meow." We named her Capuchin then and there.

It was a happy morning when I saddled up by lantern light for that last trip down to Deer Creek for winter supplies. I rode out of camp under a starless sky, leading three pack horses. In the dim light, I couldn't see Quito, the last horse, but I knew he was back there somewhere. I had a jingle bell hanging loose from his halter. As long as I heard that bell, I knew I had my outfit.

I was halfway down the mountain before a gray dawn allowed me a forecast of the weather for the day. Low-hanging leaden clouds spread from horizon to horizon. A few crystal-perfect snowflakes landed on the back of my gloved hand but soon melted. Behind me the pack horses grunted occasionally and came along in a loose-jointed gait on the trail made icy by horse traffic.

That day at Deer Creek, I wanted a quick turn around for sure. But it wasn't to be. Quito had lost a shoe on the way down. It took some time to find a shoe that fit, then I borrowed some tools and nailed it on. A friend came by. I was glad to visit, but it took awhile.

The most important item on my cargo list that day was the new cook stove that we would use in our cabin, whenever we moved in. Boxed up, the unit weighed a hundred twenty pounds. That was more weight and size than I wanted on one side of a pack horse making that steep climb home.

To solve the problem, I dismantled the stove to the extent of removing stove top, lids, firebox liners, grate and oven door. The parts weighed sixty pounds, and I mantied them up in a tarp for packing. The rest of the stove I put back in the box. It would set nicely on a cargo carrier.

I picked Kyska, a big sorrel gelding, as the horse for the stove. It wasn't that the stove was so heavy, but the box-like unit stuck out from the horse's side farther than I like a load to do. Kyska was going to have to be a master at balancing as he scratched his way up that icy trail.

I packed the main part of the stove on Kyska's left side. I knew that the trees that crowded the trail would be on his right on the trip home. I packed the stove parts on his right and tossed a sack of mail between the crossbucks of the pack saddle. After draping a tarp over the top, I threw my diamond. The first horse was ready to go.

We had purchased some thirty-gallon galvanized garbage cans for rodent-proof storage on the mountain. I packed one on the left side of both Topper and Quito. I filled the cans to the brim with the last packages to come in the mail. Those two horses carried general cargo on their right sides. Soon I had three horses packed and strung out for the mountain.

As we trailed across the flats in the foothills, the wind came up, and it started to snow. The horses bowed their necks and turned their heads. They were good horses, long of leg and deep in the heart, with enough withers to hold a saddle. In a couple of days, I would pull their shoes and turn them loose in that big pasture for the winter.

It was dark by the time we got to the foot of Gunshot Trail. I stopped to let the horses rest. No matter how full his belly is, a horse is always ready to eat. My four dropped their heads and pawed through the snow for dry grass. I bolted down a cold sandwich and sipped hot tea the thoughtful lady at Deer Creek had put in my thermos.

Continuing up, we climbed and rested. The horses had made that trip many times before, in daylight and dark. They knew the trail well and knew our customary places to stop.

I met no other late travelers. Hunters had pulled their elk camps and packed off the mountain days ago.

By the time we slipped through the timber below the CH Rim, it was as dark as the inside of a cow. Bridger knew where he was heading, and I let him pick his way. Behind us, I could tell when the pack on Kyska's right side lightly scraped a tree. Topper and Quito heard the cue and moved over to avoid the tree.

About halfway through the timber, I didn't know when to duck for a low limb, and I lost my cap. I dismounted and felt around for it on my hands and knees, but couldn't find it. Fortunately, I had a flashlight in my saddlebag. With the light, I located it easily.

In the beam of the flashlight, I could see the heavily falling snow melting on the warm bodies of the horses. I walked along the string checking their loads. Cinches had some slack, but the diamonds were still snug.

I got aboard Bridger and called down the line to the pack horses. When I started up the timber-lined trail, I felt Kyska coming along with slack in his lead rope.

When we pulled out in the open of Mule Deer Park, I shined the flashlight back along the pack string to see how they were doing. I sucked in my breath. Kyska was the only pack horse I had!

I tied Bridger and Kyska to trees at the edge of the timber and back-tracked down the trail. I couldn't have made it without the aid of the flashlight. The wind had increased to such force, it was blowing snow across the trail, even in the timber.

At length I found the other two horses. There stood Topper and Quito, waiting patiently at the place where I had stopped for my cap. I guess the noise of the wind in the tall pines and spruces must have drowned out my voice when I called to the string to come along. Thus, when Kyska had moved up fast to keep up with my saddle horse, Topper had hung back. The breakaway rope had parted, and the two were left behind.

I gathered up Topper's lead rope and started the walk up the winding trail. Out in the open, I put the outfit together and got mounted.

Mule Deer Park, which slants toward the bottom of the draw, has always been a slippery place when wet with rain or snow. That night was no exception. Wet snow balled up the horses' feet so the winter calks weren't doing any good. I felt Bridger slipping and sliding in the dark. Behind him, I heard the pack horses having trouble keeping their footing. In spite of the cutting wind, my body felt far from cold. I would be glad to reach camp.

Then at once, it seemed, the wind abated. The snow came down in gentle swirls. At first the clouds parted just enough for the stars to peek through here and there. Aloft the wind was still strong, and it herded scattered clouds before it. Soon the skies were clear, and moon and stars lent light to the open park.

Toward the east, Orion, the hunter, kept his station in the sky as he has since time before memory. I knew the way home. And I knew my horses knew the way home. But it was comforting to have Orion up there to tell me I was right.

Sometime later I hailed the camp as I topped a ridge and started down a draw. Skipper answered my call by barking like a watchdog, then kept his silence. From past experience, I knew he was listening and waiting. At the end of the string, Quito, nearing home, shook his head and danced down the hill. His jingle bell sent a message to Skipper's ear. Soon the dog was bouncing happily alongside as we filed through the gateway Mary had opened.

By lantern light, we unpacked, unsaddled, and curried. We grained the horses and turned them loose. Down the slope, we heard the bell of the loose horses who had remained at home that day. In a moment, the horses would nicker a greeting to each other, then join up and snort and prance around.

Mary and I walked toward the lit-up tent. The smell of pine smoke, fresh coffee, and hot food was a greeting in itself.

We paused and looked up. From out of the north came a

soul-stirring call that spoke of wildness and freedom and high adventure. It was the quavering honk of migrating geese. Music of a sort, if you listened that way. With confidence they flew due south, straight across the moon in a fluid Vee.

Life Under Canvas

W E HEAR A LOT about togetherness these days. Well, all I can say is that you don't know anything about togetherness until you've spent the winter in a ten-by-twelve wall tent. That is, with a wife and a dog and cat. But, you know, thinking back on it, I don't recall that it was anything but a happy time.

We felt we already had a good home under canvas. But we did a few things to make it a better winter camp.

I ran some small poles along the inside of the tent walls at eaves' height. From the poles, we hung tarps and cow hides to form sort of a double wall. Where the pole ran behind the stove, I drove in some nails. It proved a handy place to hang wet jackets and gloves.

I put a vertical prop under the ridge pole right up against the bed. It not only supported the ridge when snow lay heavy, but after I drove in some nails, we used the prop as another place to hang stuff.

There was room between the foot of the bed and the tent wall. I built a set of shelves for that space. We covered the sod floor with old saddle blankets and the remaining cow hide. We hung a tarp inside the tent flaps in front to act as a storm door.

There was no shortage of snow. We used some of it to build a wall all around the outside of the tent at eaves' height. It made a good windbreak.

We didn't have much room for hanging oil paintings, but we did have a saddle shop calendar with some fine Charlie Russell prints.

Mary added the final woman's touch to our home. It came in the form of a potted ivy, complete with plastic cover. Mary nursed that plant through the winter, below zero nights and all.

o o o

Our coldest morning that winter was twenty-eight degrees below zero. And we had many mornings when the temperature hung at fifteen below to twenty below until almost noon. Mary and I weren't strangers to weather like that. It was typical of the working conditions a rancher operating in the Rocky Mountain West contends with almost any winter. Some are colder. But even on days like that, there are jobs outside that will keep a person warm. For one thing, I could peel logs. And for another, I always figured that below zero weather was a good time to top off our stacks of split firewood.

On the days of coldest temperature, Mary proclaimed a baking day. A wall tent of white canvas is never a dismal place. And our little Sims stove never found it a chore to keep the place warm. In that setting, Mary mixed and kneaded and let rise the dough for bread and rolls. The folding oven she set on top of the stove only baked two loaves at a time. And she had to watch it closely to see that it didn't get too hot. However, Mary always seemed to get the job done. And she whistled and sang all the time she was getting it done.

On our regular working days, Mary quit early enough to go inside to prepare supper. By the time I got in, she had the wash-up water hot and handy. Then I shaved while we listened to evening news. Whatever Mary had for supper always tasted good to me.

People have often asked, "What could you possibly do in the evening?"

Well, Mary and I talked a lot. On everything from philosophizing on issues past and present to our specific plans for the next day. We recalled to mind friends we had known through the years and the bearing those people had on our lives. Reminiscing about our earlier years, when our children were growing up, was a topic we returned to often.

We read almost every night and enjoyed the music that came out of our cassette player. We wrote letters, even though they might not get mailed for four to six months. And we re-read letters we received from the special people in our lives. Above all, we enjoyed that exclusive feeling that came from sharing a unique adventure.

We found it best for body and soul to have a regular scheduled work day. It was the only way we were ever going to build a house of logs and get moved in.

In the morning, I was the first to get up and stir around. The tent was as cold as a deep freeze when I crawled out. But not long after I fired up the Sims stove, my teeth usually stopped chattering. Then I answered Mary's question about what temperature showed on the outside thermometer. Some mornings I figured it was best not to tell her.

I put water on to heat for coffee, cereal and washing-up. Next I hung our clothes on a line over the stove to thaw out. Then I hopped back in bed. Invariably, Mary let out a yelp when my cold body made contact with her warm body. She didn't think it funny when I laughed. After awhile Mary got up and cooked breakfast. It was a pretty good arrangement.

ø ø ø

Laundry day at our camp was anything but typical. It started the day Mary found the stove that first fall. She had been poking around on a hillside not far below our camp, looking for gizzard stones. There, half-hidden under pine needles, Mary made a greater discovery—a small, rusty cast iron stove. But to Mary it was a household gem of important potential. How it got there is anyone's guess.

Mary cleaned out the silt and pine needles. Then she rolled the stove up the hill, over and over, until she reached camp. Her eyes sparkled with enthusiasm as she told me she now had a hot water heater for her open air laundry. Mary enlisted my help, and we set up the plant conveniently near the spring.

Now, well into the winter, with snow piled up around it, the plant worked full force one day a week.

On laundry day, I started the fire in the stove and fetched all the water Mary would need for the project. I put a section of stovepipe on the stove so it would draw better. After it was going good, Mary fed small chunks of wood to the fire by simply dropping them down the stovepipe. That left the stove top free to set two buckets of water to heat.

When the plant was in full operation, the steam rose high in the cold air. Mary was proud of her project. She talked of putting up a sign: MARY'S WET WASH. She had a scrub board made from a piece of corrugated roofing she found at the old cow camp. The rubber plunger—often referred to as a plumber's helper—turned out to be her faithful helper.

It was a matter of scrub, plunge, wring, hang up. Mary wore woolen gloves to hang the clothes on the line. She dried the gloves near the stove between batches. To keep the clothespins from freezing, she soaked them in salt-water brine.

Drifting snow was a problem that first winter. It seemed I never had a path cleared under the line when Mary wanted to hang up wet clothes. That never bothered her. She simply buckled on her snowshoes and kept the project moving.

I remember one of my shirts was badly oil-stained. Mary

put it in an extra bucket to soak. Before she got around to work on the shirt again, it became frozen fast in solid ice.

Mary has never been one to fret about unimportant things. She set the bucket with the captive shirt to one side. Soon it was buried under a couple of feet of snow. Once in awhile, Mary would make reference to the shirt as an April shirt. She had good reason. It was late April before she got the thing thawed out and hung on the line.

ø ø ø

We were pretty busy that first winter, and some things just didn't get done. Like me getting a haircut, for instance. It got to the point where Mary said I looked like a Rambouillet sheep. The next day she started to shear.

Mary set me atop a chopping block in the middle of the tent with the official barber's cape pinned around me. At my urgent request, she warmed up the hand clippers and scissors. Then she went to work.

It was about thirty years ago that Mary started giving me haircuts. I had gone to work for a cow outfit owned by The Brothers Three. They were big and tough. Fine men. But they all had the same middle name: WORK.

I came home one night and told Mary the only way I was ever going to get time off for a haircut was to quit. In the next mail, she ordered a barber outfit from Montgomery Ward. I remember it came in a green box with a book of instructions on cutting hair.

Mary has always been ready to try something new—on somebody else. I'll never forget that first haircut. It was tug and pull for over an hour. Mary seemed to hold up under the stress better than I did.

Each time Mary gives me a haircut, she always brings up the subject of how much I owe her. I've never checked her figures, but she tells me that through the years she has given me $1,260.75 worth of professional services. She always adds, "That doesn't include interest and taxes."

There are times when the truth is cruel. I don't know why Mary has to remind me that when she started giving me haircuts my hair was wavy and almost red. After a pause, she says, "It's so white now—what's left of it."

At the end of the session in the tent that day, Mary undraped me. With a flourish she handed me a small mirror. As I examined her work, I had to admit she had improved through the years. I've always believed that worthy people should be complimented. I told her that it was nice we didn't have to use so many band-aids now.

ø ø ø

It seems most people who live in houses with doors and latches also have a dog or a cat. We had both, and we had one

advantage over people who live in houses. That is, we never had to get up at night to let the dog or cat in or out. They just made their way between the flaps of the tent as they pleased. After they had made their passage, the folds of canvas fell neatly together.

At times, we did have a problem with Skipper. Whenever the coyotes came by at night, they always stopped for a spell. I believe they considered it an interesting diversion to stir up the dog for awhile. One night the coyotes stopped by as usual. Skipper's keen ears quickly caught their yipping and howling. The dog sprang from his rug under our bed. Barking furiously, as though he was going right out to tear the coyotes apart, he charged to the front of the tent.

But did he go out into the cold of the winter night to tear them apart? Never. Skipper just stuck his head out through the folds of the canvas and left his hind end in. There he stood, barking and howling back at the coyotes, and all the time letting cold air into the tent. No amount of hollering from our bed dislodged the dog. He would neither go on out nor come back in.

By then I was furious myself. I got out of bed and went to the front of the tent. There, I poked my head out through the flaps and hollered at the coyotes to the full capacity of my lungs. Below me, at almost ground level, Skipper still had his head out and was doing his share. By that time, Mary was stirred up, too. I was afraid she might boot Skipper and me out front with the coyotes. Finally the coyotes drifted off, and Mary and I and Skipper went to sleep. Capuchin, our kitten, was a sound sleeper. Even though the episode was repeated throughout the winter, I don't remember a time when the fuss made the kitten stir from the foot of the bed.

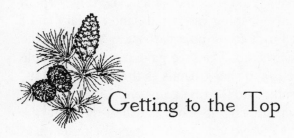

Getting to the Top

I N WINTER, THE TOP of the mountain is such a peaceful place. It was with reluctance that I started our chain saw at the beginning of any working day. But start it I must because I had found another use for the saw. Fortunately, our saw is quieter than most.

As time went along, I made better saddle notches and got them set down in shorter time. This was due, in large part, to the help I got from the chain saw. I learned to use the saw to give the right shape to a notch, almost as one would use a sander. To get the proper effect from the saw, I used a chain that had been worn so much the cutting teeth were small. Thus, the bite they took was lessened.

When the logs were notched, I positioned and spiked log after log. It was a great day when I could no longer look over the top log of the cabin wall. Early in the fall, I had selected and put aside the logs I planned to use for the two plates and the ridge. They were the cream of the crop.

The plates were the longest logs I had used so far. They would extend well out in front for the porch. We allowed for a three foot overhang in back. We notched and spiked down the plates and added a cross log at each end. Next we built the gables for a quarter-pitched roof.

Now came an event of real importance, sort of a milestone in the building of any cabin. It was time to put the ridgelog in place near the top of the gable. The ridge would be the longest and heaviest log we would handle. Mary and I used some half-inch rope to rig up a parbuckle and rolled the timber into place with ease. Then we gave out with a couple of good cowboy yells and shook hands as though we had just driven the golden spike into the first transcontinental railroad.

I spiked down the ridgelog and finished building the gable to the peak. Now we could select logs for rafters and get them ready to put in place.

Using the chain saw, I flattened each rafter on top to make it ready to receive roof boards. Rafters had a three foot overhang at the eaves. Later, that place would provide shelter for gear we would hang from pegs driven into the outside of the log walls.

The rafters went up quickly. Mary poked the ends up until I could reach them. I spiked them down on the places I had marked on the plate and the ridgelog. It seemed we made giant strides forward that day. The building looked less box-like. With the roof timbers reaching out front, back and sides, it looked as if our house wanted to grow.

During this time we had snowfall two or three times a week. Keeping paths and work areas clean was a never-ending job. And, of course, some of the snow fell inside the cabin. That was the first place Mary tackled after a fresh snow. I remember the morning right after we got the rafters up. Mary paused in her task and called out the door.

"Mark," she said, "I really belong to an exclusive club."

I looked up from the path I was clearing. "What do you mean?"

"Well, I bet I'm the only woman, east or west of the Mississippi, who's shoveling snow out of the inside of her house this morning."

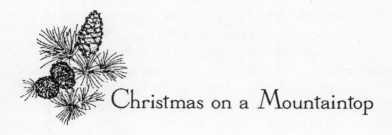 Christmas on a Mountaintop

SMELLS OF BACON and eggs filled the tent as Mary and I talked and sipped our second cups of coffee. A few minutes earlier, I had poked my head out through the tent flaps. In the beam of the flashlight, I could see four inches of new snow, and the thermometer showed the temperature hanging at zero. Overhead in the pre-dawn sky, a host of stars showed dimly. But just above the eastern horizon, Vega still held big and bright.

Mary looked at me over the brim of her cup.

"Let's go get those nails," she said. "It'll be a fine day for snowshoeing, and I think it'll do us good to get away from camp for awhile."

The date was December 24. In past years, Mary had always seemed especially busy on that day. Fixing this. Fixing that. But this year, living in a tent, things were probably already as fixed as they could be.

I thought back to one of the trips up the mountain with the pack horses. I remembered a box marked CHRISTMAS DECORATIONS. That box had been around the house at Deer Creek a long time. Mary had always considered Christmas decorating one of her important jobs. But this year she didn't have a house to decorate. I felt badly about that, because I had practically promised Mary we would be moved into our new log home by Christmas.

The box of nails Mary referred to was at the old cow camp. A rancher friend had left them there for us when he went by on his way to his hunting camp.

Soon we were making tracks for the cow camp. The zero degree temperature made for good snowshoeing. The fresh snow was light and fluffy—not at all the kind to stick to your webs. Underneath, a foot and a half of settled snow gave some support to our snowshoes.

I broke trail for Mary. Skipper followed close at her heels, sometimes stepping on her snowshoes.

We were glad to top out on the timbered divide. From there on, the tree-lined trail was on the downslope all the way to the cow camp.

In the forest it was common to find gray, lifeless lodgepole pines leaning against tall, gothic-spired alpine firs. Now, in a light wind, pine rubbed against fir, creating moans and groans and screeches. Mary said Big Foot was calling her.

Clearly, we didn't have exclusive possession of the mountain. It was more that our neighbors owned the mountain and were sharing it with us.

Overhead, a couple of ravens let out a hoarse croak and soared below a blue sky. Then they put on a display of graceful aerobatics, not at all in keeping with the coarse features of such a short-necked, heavy-billed bird.

Coyote tracks showed ahead on the fresh snow. After awhile, the sign told the story that the coyote had turned off the trail and had followed the indistinct tracks of a mouse through a tangle of downed timber.

To the north, we heard the hammering of a woodpecker's beak against the trunk of a dry lodgepole. A pine squirrel looked down from the swaying branch of a spruce. That day, he was willing to keep his silence and just watch the parade of people and dog go by.

Whenever Mary and I travel the winding trails of the high country, we communicate by sign rather than by voice. So it was that morning.

Movement below caught my eye just as we started to descend to where the trail widened to form a pint-sized meadow. I stopped and signaled Mary to come forward slowly.

For the next five minutes we watched the antics of an ermine. The animal was snow-white except for his black nose and eyes and the black tip of his tail. With quick movements, he bounced his long body and short legs along the top of the snow. After stopping to look around, he dived beneath the snow, traveled out of sight for a few feet, and  returned to the top again. Always alert. Always quick. He checked the base of the trees, then disappeared into the snow and returned again.

Skipper was no problem during this show. His ears were keen, but his eyes were lacking, especially for focusing on a white animal moving quickly against snow. Finally however, he whined impatiently. The ermine had been sniffing around the base of a leaning pine snag when he heard Skipper whine. Like a flash of white, he went aloft. Carefully, we moved forward for a closer look.

From a jutting limb, the ermine looked down on us, his black eyes showing neither fear nor hate, but only interest. We moved down the trail and let the ermine be.

Tracks of snowshoe hares were along the trail, as they usually are after a fresh snow. The tracks are far more common than the sight of the animals themselves, since they move about mostly at night. Nevertheless, I bet more than one big, white rabbit lay huddled close to the ground, in perfect camouflage, and watched us file by.

We hadn't seen any elk on the mountain in a long time and didn't expect to see any now. We knew they had drifted down to lower country. It's only occasionally that we see moose. There isn't enough willow around to make for ideal moose habitat.

As we crossed the horse pasture surrounding the cow camp, we saw three big mule deer bucks. They were nibbling on the tender ends of Douglas fir branches. We wondered what possessed them to stay in the high country during the time of deep snow. Of course, I suppose there are people who wondered what possessed Mary and me to stay in the high country during the time of deep snow.

Moving on, we heard the weak whistles of a pine grosbeak coming from the top of a blue spruce. We like to see that red-topped, red-fronted bird around because he adds color to the winter scene.

We hung our snowshoes on a nail by the cabin door, and I shoveled the snow away to clear the entry. I had to put a shoulder to the door and push hard to get it open. The floor boards had buckled in places, so the door dragged a mite in summer. In the winter, when the snow blew in under the door and formed a small drift behind it, it dragged a mite more.

Mary got a fire going in the old Monarch cook stove and started poking around in the tin cupboard.

I looked down toward the spring and saw four or five feet of snow drifted over it. I decided snow-water would be the quickest way to get hot coffee. I filled a big metal dishpan with snow and placed it on the stove.

Soon Mary was stirring up a batch of hotcake mix. It wasn't what we usually had for lunch. But the cabin seemed to have more pancake flour around than four cowboys could eat in four years.

After lunch, we sat at the little table and sipped on hot

coffee. I told Mary stories about the old cabin that she already knew and would likely hear again.

Here and there on the logs inside, visitors had carved initials and dates. The more ambitious types carved a full name, such as Porcupine Red or Bull Elk Pete. The logs held a record of the range riders who had whiled away the time after supper and of the time they lived in that cabin.

Other visitors also left their marks. Like the black bear that left muddy paw prints on the window panes. That was when a lad by the name of Will rode for the grazing association.

It seems one evening Will was eating supper at the little table. Long ago someone had put that table in the right place. As he ate, a man could look out the window and admire the distant peaks.

From what I heard, Will was giving equal time to the view and to what was on his supper plate. After a turn at meat and potatoes, Will raised his head and found his view blocked. There stood a big black bear rubbing his muddy front paws on the window panes. Will let out a yell and went over backwards in his chair, landing with a crash on the floor.

I guess it took awhile for Will to get himself gathered up to peek out the window. By that time, the bear was lumbering down across the creek headed for tall, dense timber. Will went back to eating supper, hoping the bear wouldn't be back to block his view.

BEAR TRACKS

The last time I heard of Will, he was judging the bronc riding at a rodeo. I wonder if he ever thinks of the bear who came to supper.

I had stayed in that cabin one fall twenty-two years earlier. My job was to help Old Jed gather cattle and get them pushed off the mountain.

Old Jed wasn't much bigger than a pint of Jim Beam, but he was tougher than rawhide. He had three pinto geldings that he rode, along with some horses from the cattlemen's association. Those pintos were like Jed—small but tough. Chasing cows, Jed rode those horses in places where mountain goats fear to tread.

In the evenings I listened to Jed's stories about following the roundup wagons of big outfits up north. Or how he drove a four-horse hitch down into a canyon that had never seen wheel tracks before.

There is one thing I remember most about my days with Jed. In fact, I can't forget it.

Jed came up the mountain in June, maybe a week or so ahead of the cattle. When he reached camp, he started cooking up a big pot of stew. Old Jed never ran out. He just kept adding to it. That stew pot never left its place at the back of the stove until Jed went off the mountain with the cattle in October.

I remember waking up that fall while it was still dark. I picked up a boot and let it fall to the floor with a thump. After awhile Jed got up and started breakfast. I smiled in pleasant anticipation. It was the only time I didn't have to eat stew.

But now, I saw Mary was getting restless. I had gone through my stories about the cow camp. Maybe Mary thought I would start over again.

"Mark," she said, "this is great, but I really should be getting back. You know, getting supper started and things. Would you mind if I left you with the dishes and headed for camp?"

"That would be fine," I replied. "You take off. It gets dark so early now."

Mary zipped up her parka and went out the door. I watched her put on her snowshoes. With Skipper at her heels, she soon shuffled across the pasture on our packed trail. At the rate she was going, I was glad that I didn't have to catch up with her.

I checked the water in the dishpan. It was hot. But if I was going to do a proper job of cleaning those dishes, I decided it would be better if the water was hotter. Besides, there was a little coffee left.

I refilled my cup, sat down at the little table and looked out the window. I never got tired of looking at those tall peaks.

I thought about when I was in the fourth grade and my teacher used to shake her head.

"Mark," she said, "you'll never amount to anything. All you want to do is look out the window and daydream."

I thought about that for awhile. Then I got up and washed the dishes.

Before I pulled out for home, I had another chore to do. I poked my head out the door. At the top of my voice I yelled, "Come on horses. Come on." I tried to make it sound like I did when I stayed at the cow camp in years past. My voice echoed back, the sound filling the open space between rocky crag and forest wall.

I yelled again. I was glad there wasn't anyone around to hear me. After all, there hadn't been a horse on the mountain in well over a month.

I went back into the cabin and picked up two leftover hotcakes from the back of the stove. I went outside and watched and waited. My short vigil was rewarded. From across the creek, two gray jays came gliding in on silent wings. They landed close by my feet. Hopping around, they talked to me like a couple of barnyard hens. They knew that horses being called and leftover hotcakes went together. I tossed each bird a prize. They accepted and flew away.

ø ø ø

The soft edge of early darkness was just closing in as I followed Mary's snowshoe tracks down the hill. When I hailed the camp, Skipper barked as though he meant business. When I called again, he bounded up the trail to meet me.

I slipped off the backpack at the outdoor workbench. I was glad to get those nails home. Next time I would get them home by pack horse.

White smoke was lifting above the lit-up tent. Outside, from a pole stuck in a snowbank, hung a light I had never seen before. It was a glass-enclosed candle lantern. Inside, a red candle burned brightly. As I brushed through the tent flaps, sleigh bells made cheery sounds.

Inside, Mary stood with her feet close together, her hands at her sides. She had a new red shirt on and had fixed her hair up nicely. She looked as though she was about to recite a poem at a schoolhouse Christmas program.

Mary's eyes sparkled. She could no longer contain herself. Her special-time, little-girl laugh bubbled out as tinkling music. With a bound she reached me and bussed me soundly. I looked up. From the ridgepole hung a sprig of mistletoe.

Mary stepped aside. With a sweep of her hand, she invited me to look. A miniature Christmas tree of perfect proportions stood on a shelf at the foot of our bed. The tree sparkled with all the decorations a small tree could hold.

Small touches of Christmas showed throughout the tent. Single poinsettias were pinned here and there to the roof. Clusters of sparkling balls hung from the ridge, silver icicles were everywhere.

The square of plywood that served as our table was already set for the evening meal. On its center, a candle burned in a wine bottle encrusted with wax drippings of

bright colors. I knew the candle holder well. It had taken well over thirty years to achieve that look of antiquity.

That evening after supper, we talked. Eventually, we spoke aloud about something that was on both our minds. This would be the first time we hadn't had at least one of our children home for Christmas. But fledglings grow up and leave the nest. Sometimes they fly to far off places. Ours did.

I thought back to Christmas Eves at Deer Creek. Even after the boys were a head taller than me, and our daughter was almost as tall as Mary, they still wanted me to read to them on Christmas Eve. They would stretch out on the floor, with the backdrop of blazing fire and empty stockings hanging from the hand-hewn mantle.

It seemed the best stories came out of *Christmas Ideals.* They were the traditional kind. I would read until my voice became hoarse. Invariably I ended the session with Saint Luke's account of the birth of Christ. They were good times.

ø ø ø

I awoke the next morning to the sound of joyous music filling the candle-lit tent. Mary hustled about. She cut quite a figure with her pajamas tucked into her snow boots and with puffs of steam coming out of the fur-trimmed hood of her parka. Already a fire roared in the Sims stove.

Mary's face beamed. "Merry Christmas, Mark."

I rubbed my eyes. "Merry Christmas, Mary. But what are you doing up? That's my job to light the fire."

"Oh, this is just for today—my Christmas present to you," Mary came back.

As it turned out, that wasn't the only Christmas present Mary had to surprise me. After breakfast, we opened presents I didn't even know were on the mountain. Family and friends were so good to us. His tail wagging furiously, Skipper stood by for the opening of each package. Capuchin, our kitten, played with all the tissue paper that fell to the floor.

Christmas dinner was a grand affair. Mary covered our plywood table with a proper Christmas tablecloth, with napkins to match. A red candle added another festive touch.

A month earlier, Mary had split a turkey down the middle, putting the two parts in our meat cache where they quickly froze. Mary had resurrected one for this holiday meal. I was amazed that we had all the trimmings to go with the turkey. Mary likes to hide things here and there. Then she brings them to the surface as a surprise at the proper time.

As we sat and talked after supper, we were both overcome with a deep feeling of contentment and thankfulness. The best Christmas present we had received was just being up on the mountain. We enjoyed a way of life that we had looked forward to for many years. Each day brought us as much fulfillment as any person could hope for. Best of all, we found that fulfillment by working together.

Moving In

W HEN I GOT THE RIDGE and the rafters up with Mary's help, I felt our house was taking on some planned shape. We still didn't have a roof over our heads, but that was soon to come.

I shoveled and swept snow off the pile of one-by-eight boards that had been flown in by helicopter earlier.

I set up sawhorses near the cabin where we measured, squared, and cut. I passed the boards up to Mary for nailing to the rafters with twenty-penny galvanized nails.

By now, Capuchin followed Mary everywhere. With tail pointed straight up, the kitten walked along the ridgelog. After reaching the rafter that led her to the place where Mary worked, she strutted down that timber with absolute feline confidence. Occasionally, she perched on Mary's shoulder. The swinging of Mary's big framing hammer and the sound of nails being driven home never fazed the kitten.

After the roof boards were down, I installed the roof jack over the hole through which the stovepipe would pass. The conical-shaped piece was made out of heavy galvanized metal. The top of the stovepipe was three and a half feet above the ridge and carried a rain cap. Some people call that piece a Chinese hat.

At the time we were putting down the rolled roofing, morning temperatures ranged from zero to ten above. We used tarred felt paper under the ninety-pound roofing. Temperature was no problem for the tar paper. But the low temperature was surely a problem for the ninety-pound. It didn't take much handling to tear it. So we warmed it alongside the stove in the tent to help soften it. Later, we'd set it outside for the sun to take some of the stiffness out.

We used an old pair of tin shears for cutting the material. A gallon can of hot water proved helpful for that job. Before we started to cut, we'd immerse the shears in the hot water. They cut smoother then, leaving no cracks along the cut edge.

It was a happy day for Mary when she drove the last roofing nail through that heavy rolled roofing. She climbed down the ladder and went inside the cabin. Mary walked around looking up at the underside of the roof. No daylight showed. Mary smiled. "Now," she said, "I'm just like other women. I don't have to shovel snow out of my house anymore."

Next, I set up the stone piers for the porch sill logs. I wanted good, solid gravel to set those big, flat base rocks on. It took a bit of digging to get there. The ground was frozen rock-hard. First, I had to thaw the ground. I got a good fire going and put on some short logs, then let it smolder all night long. By morning, the ground was more willing to accept digging bar and shovel.

We mixed mortar for the job in a big bucket. The temperature was near zero at the time. I threw a handful of salt and a couple squirts of liquid detergent in the mix. I had no problem with the mortar setting up properly in that cold weather.

The porch got built. For the stair stringers, I slabbed a log on two sides and used rough two-by-tens for the steps. Pole railings dressed things up.

Earlier I had cut out a doorway. Now with the chain saw, I cut the marked openings for windows. We used rough two-by-sixes for the frames.

Money spent for good quality top flooring is money well spent, even for a log cabin. We put tarred felt paper under tongue and groove fir. It worked very well. When we'd nailed the last floor board in place, Mary and I got to our feet. We stretched to get the kinks out of our backs.

"Well, that looks pretty good," I said. "I'll start on the door in the morning."

"Door!" Mary exclaimed. "Who needs a door? It looks like the Hilton already. Let's get moved in."

The next morning, instead of building a proper door, I hung a tarp from nails driven into the door frame header, and we had a door.

Then I listened to Mary tell me where to build the bed, the table, and a couple of shelves. "Just so they won't fall down, Honey," Mary kept saying. I got the feeling she wanted me to hurry.

That first hurry-up furniture got built. Then we set up our cook stove and put the stovepipe in place up through the roof jack.

I laid split kindling in the untried firebox. Mary stood by with match in hand, ready to light off. With the drafts open, the fire soon made popping and crackling noises. Mary couldn't resist lifting one of the lids to peek in.

"Just think, Mark," she said. "A brand-new stove in a brand-new house. I think I'll go up to the tent and start packing right now."

We enjoyed cabin living from the start. Just looking around at the wall logs and up at the ridge and rafters gave us a certain satisfaction that we had never known before. Not so long ago, those house timbers had been standing dead trees or windfalls up on the hill. Working together, we had put a roof over our heads. Already we thought of it as home.

I did get around to building a door. It was of rather

heavy construction, worthy of being hung in the doorway of a house of logs. We planned it as a Dutch door, but I built it and hung it in one piece. With a hand saw I cut it in half, and it fit just right.

Surely a Dutch door fits the mood of a wilderness cabin. When the weather is right and the top half of the door is open, it makes a person feel much closer to the country around him.

Another thing Mary liked about our Dutch door is that in the summer she could close the bottom half to keep the dogs out if she wanted. Yet with the top half open, chickadees and hummingbirds could fly in for a visit if they wished. Hummingbirds actually came so close as to try to get nectar from Mary's pink lipstick.

 Snow Eater

SWINGING ONE SNOWSHOE ahead of the other, I fairly skimmed across the crusted snow. High up and behind me, a three-quarter moon flooded the open park through which I traveled. Along the fringe of the timber bordering the park, a light wind sighed among the pines and spruces, gently moving their tops across a star-flecked sky. The air had just enough nip to make me want the hood of my parka to cover my ears. All these things together filled me with an exhilaration that was a pleasure to feel. The time was one hour past midnight.

Traveling by snowshoe in the hours between midnight and dawn was not one of the things that I routinely did. However, sometimes in late winter, weather conditions were not ideal for snowshoe travel. Even at eight thousand feet, the midday temperature can be so high that the heat makes the snow heavy and sticky. Every time a person lifts a snowshoe to push it ahead, he also lifts a load of snow. Those conditions slow down a web-footed traveler and tax his strength.

When it became necessary for me to make a quick trip to the low country and to town, I decided to travel during the colder nighttime hours. This far, the thought seemed to be a good one. Yesterday's sun had warmed the surface of a two to three foot snow pack and had melted it some. When the chill of the night came on, the snow's surface crusted and hardened. My snowshoes broke through just enough to keep me from sliding around.

Swinging along on the downhill grade, I made good time, and I didn't have to work hard to do it. A great horned owl glided by on silent wings not far above my head. Likely, his mate was already sitting on a clutch of eggs and now waited for him to return with the fresh meat of a snowshoe hare. Over toward the Dutch Oven Country, a couple of coyotes let me know they were stirring about. Not quite in harmony, they sent mournful music toward the moon.

Leaving Mule Deer Park, I entered the timber below the CH Rim where tall pine and spruce shut off the light of the moon. There the snow was not crusted, and my webs sank deeper. In the dim light, I used my flashlight to check my course on the unbroken, little-used track. After awhile, I joined up with the main trail sidling down Gunshot Canyon. There, helped along by the fall of the land, I was able to reach out in long, ground-covering strides. The snowshoe-marked trail fell steadily behind me. At length I broke out on a viewpoint from where I could look down on the dim features of snow-clad foothills and creek-bottom valleys.

In the east, a still hidden sun-ball had just started to put a blush on the open sky above it. As I continued on toward the lower country, the early light of dawn became stronger. Soon I recognized places and things for what they were.

Objects moving up Ponderosa Creek now clearly showed up as a herd of elk. In keeping with long habit, they had grazed the meadows and lower pastures of the ranch that night. In this country, a rancher's cows have to share their winter grass, and often their hay, with the elk and the deer.

Off the trail, I leaned against an age-scarred ponderosa pine and watched the elk come closer. Using my small binoculars, I made a rough count. Close to two hundred head, I figured. On they came, cows and calves and bulls. Most of the older bulls and a few of the younger bulls had already shed their antlers. Some of last year's yearlings would not lose their spikes until April or even early May. Probably only a few calves were still getting their mother's milk. Even so, some sounds of cow-calf talk drifted up the slope. With their paunches full, the elk continued to move higher. In an hour, they would be bedded down in the timber on the steep face of the mountain. There, they would chew their cuds and rest.

That evening when the soft shadows of early darkness settled on the foothills and meadows, the elk would get up and stretch. Some would reach up with a hind foot and scratch for ticks behind their ears. Then, as if on signal, they would drift off the face of the mountain to drink along Ponderosa Creek and to graze the meadows and lower pastures of the ranch once again.

Wide awake and thinking of breakfast, I shuffled on down to Deer Creek. The men had already gone out to work, but the good lady there cooked me ham and eggs and gave me news of the place.

That day I hustled around town and got a lot of things done, but not enough. Mary had predicted that. She said, "You'll meet up with some of those old cowmen and get to talkin' too long."

The next morning I carried on. Sidewalk travel made my feet ache, and I risked my life crossing the streets. Toward noon I ran into another rancher friend, and we had lunch together. Among other things, he told me the weather forecast called for a change, with the prospect of snow-melting Chinook winds coming off the mountain the next day. No matter, I thought. I would be home by then. My plan was to travel in the dark again, after the nighttime chill had firmed up the snow to furnish support for my webs.

That evening after dark, the temperature dropped on schedule, and the snow firmed up as it should. I pointed my snowshoes toward home, uphill all the way. But my pack was light—just twenty-five pounds of mail, a couple of sandwiches, and a box of chocolate-covered mints for Mary. With my spirits high, I felt I was ready for whatever the night should send my way.

One step at a time, making good use of the packed trail I made coming down, I started to climb the steep trail leading toward the high country. The effort soon warmed me. I traveled with my parka open, letting body heat escape as it would.

I stopped and rested at places like Rattlesnake Switch-back and Grouse Dance Point, places where we always let our horses blow for a few minutes or so. At Last Chance Rock, I slipped off my pack and ate the light lunch I had brought along. I don't know who named that point in some year long past, but surely it was the last chance to turn and look at the open country below.

From Last Chance to the top of Gunshot Canyon, the passage is through thick timber where Douglas fir and Engelmann spruce claw for a toehold on the steep hillsides.

I shouldered my pack and entered the dark, ascending aisle. Looking up and beyond the tops of tall trees, I saw only a handful of stars. Closed in the way I was, I could expect no help from the light of the moon. I used my flashlight to show me the way.

The trail I traveled sees little sun in the winter. Whatever snowfall it receives usually remains the whole season through. Slanting drifts crossed the trail, two to five feet deep. Now my rest stops came closer together. Pausing, I leaned against the trunk of a tree, sensing the unusual quiet of the night. I listened for any sounds of moving water that might come up from that deep, black gash that was Gunshot Canyon. I untied the drawstring of the hood of my parka and pulled it back. With my ears uncovered, I cocked my head and listened intently. What I heard was not the sound of open water.

The sound came from a long way off and not from the canyon bottom. I turned my head and looked up the dark, forested face of the mountain. The noise came as a hollow roar, increasing in volume as it moved my way. I strained my eyes as well as my ears, as if the sound was a tangible thing, to be seen as well as heard.

I felt a strange warmth hit my face. And the roar came on. The tops of spruce and fir whipped violently, as the wind struck as almost a solid thing, buffeting, bending, breaking. Evergreen needles filled the air and hit my face. Small branches flew by, close above my head. The front wall of the air mass moved on, increasing in heat and speed as it continued its wild plunge down the face of the mountain. Chinook! And ahead of schedule at that.

The Indians living along the eastern slope of the Rocky Mountains called the Chinook wind the Snow Eater. They had good reason. The rise in air temperature can be dramatic, as much as twenty to thirty degrees in fifteen minutes, causing snow to melt away at a rapid rate.

I looked up the trail and continued on. The wind still came, warm and gusty. My opened parka whipped around me. At once it seemed, the snow became heavy and sticky, clinging to my webs as I started a new step. As the surface of the snow melted, the once-clear imprint my webs had made on my trip down the mountain became harder to see. Soon the trail became track free.

Things were not working out the way I had planned. If the Chinook hadn't moved in early, my trail back up the mountain would still have been hard-packed. As every minute passed, the snow became more "rotten," giving way to snow-shoe pressure. I sank through a foot of mushy snow at every step. The effort required to lift a snow-laden web taxed my strength. My feet were like lead. My leg muscles ached.

My hope was that the Chinook had not come down from aloft until it was over the face of the mountain. It could be that, untouched by the warm breath of the Snow Eater, my trail on top was still cold and hard-packed. That thought encouraged me on.

I came to one of the few places where the afternoon sun bore down on the trail. There, the snow lay at more of a slant, probably not over eight inches at the edge of the trail. I moved over. Now when the snow gave way, I would not have to go so far to hit bottom.

All went well until my webs found ice under the snow. My right snowshoe slid sideways. I tangled up and fell down. I landed on my back, my feet uphill, my head hanging over the edge of the trail. Struggling, I tried to get up, but with no success. I unbuckled the waist strap on my pack, and slipped my arms free of the shoulder harness. It appeared one snow-shoe pointed north, the other south. Wiggling and grunting, I managed to unbuckle the bindings and get both feet free.

Through it all, I somehow managed to hang on to my flashlight. Now I shined it over the edge of the trail. The drop-off was sheer and a long way down. The sight was enough incentive to help me crawl away from the edge and back to the middle of the trail.

I had new batteries in my pack, so I replaced those that had grown weak. Another time, I thought, it would be better to have two flashlights in case one got lost in the snow. I gave some thought to camping for the night. Surely I could use the rest. But snow conditions would worsen as daylight came on. Still hoping for a cold, packed trail on top, I continued on.

The brighter light from my revitalized flashlight was a big help. I shined it up the trail. When I saw a familiar landmark, I made that my target. When I reached that point, I rested. Other times, as I forged ahead, I counted thirty steps, then paused for a rest. I was getting played out. But I was a long way from finished. The feeling in my stomach told me I was hungry. I remembered Mary telling me more than once, "You'll be hungry when you're on your deathbed."

I began to think about food. Strangely, I didn't visualize a T-bone steak or prime rib on a sizzle platter. Hot tea and cold peaches, that's what I thought about. I don't know why. Plain as day, I saw a cup of hot tea with the steam rising above it. And those cold peaches. They weren't in a dish. I had a whole can to myself. A big number two-and-one-half-size can. I saw myself take off the label so I could see the cold can sweat in a warm room then touch the can with the back of my hand to enjoy the chill even more.

Hot tea and cold peaches. I couldn't get them out of my mind. I wondered, "Am I going loco?" It couldn't be. After all, I had heard of pregnant women craving dill pickles, and no one lifted an eyebrow.

I shifted the shoulder straps on my pack to a more comfortable position and moved on. Thirty paces. Pause and rest. As far as that big rock. Pause and rest. Five minutes steady travel. Pause and rest. An hour passed by. One heavy step at a time, I slogged ahead. Give up? Not on your life! All a man had to do was to keep his eye on the next target and his mind on hot tea and cold peaches.

By now, I had gained almost four thousand feet in elevation. I had been so preoccupied with other things that I failed to notice that the wind had slackened. Aware of it now, I looked up along the trunks of tall trees. Their tops still moved across the sky, but not with the violent, lashing movements of a while ago. The wind that brushed my face was cool and gentle. Clearly, the Snow Eater, with its gluttonous appetite, was below me.

When I slipped through the timber below the CH Rim, I was assured I would have a hard-packed trail to finish out my trip. I traveled on a steady, but gradual, upgrade. After the steep grind up the Gunshot Trail, it seemed as if I was moving on the level.

I don't know where it came from, but I found new energy, and my spirits lifted. Maybe it was just shedding that closed-in feeling I had, coming up that blacked-out trail in the middle of the night. And, too, gale force winds and dense timber don't make for peace of mind.

Crossing Mule Deer Park, I had no trouble keeping to the trail. That place was big enough and open enough to gather up whatever light the moon sent down. Ahead of me, I saw a half-dozen hardy deer nipping off the new growth of juniper branches spreading above the snow. They spooked as I approached and went higher on the slope. Gathered together, they turned their mulish ears my way and watched me go by.

With the good snowshoeing conditions I had now, I didn't stop to rest as often. It was the old story—if I kept putting one snowshoe ahead of the other, I would, sooner or later, get where I wanted to go. Where I eventually wanted to go was home. But right now, this high, open divide was where I wanted to be. It was a good place to rest and take stock of the things I was privileged to see.

The wind had died down and a hush came upon the land. Dark shadows filled the canyons, and open parks showed as white islands in a sea of evergreen forest. Silhouetted against a blue-black sky, snow-capped peaks stood out clearly in the light of the moon.

Overhead, and reaching from horizon to horizon, the nighttime sky was filled with countless stars. When I contemplated the vastness of the universe, it was enough to boggle my mind. Compared to the stars, the moon is a close neighbor, a mere 250,000 miles away. Some stars are so far away we can't even see them. And the stars we can see are millions of miles away. I looked up to the western sky. There, Regulus showed big and bright. I had read once that the light from Regulus took seventy-five years to get here. A long time and a long way.

The more I thought of the enormous expanse of the universe, the more incredible it seemed. Yet I knew it was there. My mind was filled with questions. Who planned the universe? Who put it together? How long did it take? Astronomers know the stars pursue an orderly plan. With confidence, they can predict the position in the sky of any star at any time. Who sees to it that these certain stars reach the right place at the right time? Again my eyes moved slowly across the sky. The stars spoke to my heart, and I was overcome by a feeling of peace.

Once I left the divide, I had more climbing to do, but no really steep pitches. The hardest part of the trip was behind me. I followed a twisting trail through a forest where not long ago a wind of tremendous force had blown over trees and piled them one upon the other. Slipping and sliding, I crossed a rocky ridge, its lee side deep in drifted snow.

From now on, I would be on a downgrade all the way home. My pace really picked up. I reached out like a long-legged Clydesdale headed for the barn.

Above me the stars faded, and the moon slid down behind Cougar Mountain. In the east, the sky turned from blue-black to pre-dawn gray. It looked like a good day.

As I neared home, I hailed the camp. Skipper gave out with a chorus of furious barks. I called again. Soon the dog bounded up the trail. Whining and wiggling, he welcomed me back.

Ahead, I could see that Mary had a lighted Coleman lantern hanging on the porch. Knowing Mary, I bet it had been hanging there a good while. She always said she liked to give me a lighthouse to steer by.

Mary bounded down the porch steps and gave me an enthusiastic welcome home. I smiled. Suppose I had stayed away a full week!

Inside, the cabin had the appetizing aroma of a bakery. Mary had stayed up all night through, waiting for her man and baking bread and pies and cookies.

"Gosh, Mark," she said, "you must be starved. What would you like me to fix special?"

"Oh, nothing special, really," I replied. "Say, you don't happen to have some hot tea and cold peaches, do you?"

 Deep Snow & Signs of Spring

I WAS BACK HOME AND ready to work. Our next project was to build on a wing to be used as our bedroom. But weather conditions caused a delay in getting started.

My daily journal tells me that up to that time of winter we had snowfall three or four times a week. With the exception of a couple of heavy snowfalls, most of it fell in the amounts of three or four inches. Three feet of old settled snow was on the ground at the time we were about to start on the bedroom wing project.

Then it really started to snow. In fourteen days, we had seven feet of snowfall on top of the three feet already on the ground. Of course, that did not add up to ten feet of snow pack because it was always settling.

To paint a word picture of what the area around our camp looked like at this time, I'll take a few more facts from my daily journal.

During most of that time, it was typical to have three feet of snow on the cabin roof, with four feet over the porch. I tried to keep the tent roof scraped off, but sometimes that built up to two feet. The snowbank on each side of the tent was higher than the ridgepole.

I managed to keep up with the snowfall by clearing trails every day. I dared not let it build up. The banks on each side of the trails grew to the height of over six feet, so I had to toss the snow on my shovel pretty high to get rid of it. Most of the snow was the wet, sticky kind. I waxed the face of my shovel and that helped it slide off easier.

For some time, we'd had no occasion to use our log-working site which Mary and I called The High Country Log and Pole Company. I had not kept the area cleared of snow. It had built up to a depth of nearly six feet there. But, for sure, if we were to get logs and have a place to work on them, that area had to be cleared of snow. It was as simple as that. We couldn't wait for the summer sun to melt it. And it did get cleared. About that time, I told Mary that if they ever had a snow shoveling contest around here to enter my name and to bet heavily. I felt I was sure to win.

Then one morning, we woke up to find blue skies stretching from horizon to horizon. The temperature, instead of hanging close to zero, had already soared to twenty above. As the sun and the temperature lifted, so did our spirits.

We cleared more snow where we were to build the bedroom wing. Then, we built the foundation piers and allowed them to set up.

Up at The High Country Log and Pole Company, drawknives slid back and forth on still-wet logs. Peelings fell to the snow-cleared ground. Our faithful chain saw was cranked up and put to work flattening clean, white logs, top and bottom. We moved those logs down the cleared trail and stacked them near the cabin. Sill logs were laid, and our building project was underway.

For the most part, we followed the same building procedures as before. The exception was we now used tenon notches at the corners. We wanted to try a concept different from the saddle notch, and we were glad we did. Logs went up faster this time. I had learned a thing or two, and the tenon corner took less time.

The days warmed, and as they did, the snow melted. Precious water spread out on the slopes and gave nourishment to the early plants. The juncos flew up from the low country. Then, in the mornings and evenings, the call of the robins could be heard as an encouraging sign of spring. As the days of good weather continued, the warm fingers of the sun reached down and brought forth the first yellow blossoms of buttercups, below the lingering snowbanks.

I worked in shirt sleeves and enjoyed the tonic of spring air. Log after log was laid, and the walls grew higher. I found myself pausing in my work to gaze at distant ranges, and to listen to the new sounds, and to sniff the earthy smells of spring.

In spite of all that, the building progressed. There came a day when the rolled roofing was nailed in place. This time it was warm and pliable and lay flat to the boards underneath.

We installed windows and cut out the inside doorway. We built furniture and shifted it around. As we moved things to the bedroom, we gained living space in the other room.

Mary was elated. Her home had grown. Now she was the mistress of a two-room, L-shaped house built of logs.

The White Bull

B ELOW OUR CAMP a short way, the first of the lavender pasque flowers and white spring beauties were making a showing. But those early wildflowers don't need summer or even late spring. All they need is a little space on a snow-free slope and some help from the earth-warming sun.

Spring was the time of year when our daily work routine changed. As it had been in other years since we moved to the high country, we put away our building tools until deep snows returned to hold us in for the winter.

As each year passed, Mary and I had more reason to be convinced that living and working in the high country year-round was the right thing for us to do. We enjoyed the whole concept of being pioneers. Our job of taking care of cattle in the summer allowed us to learn new back country ranges. Each winter we continued to improve our cabin. It was a good life and we looked forward to spring.

As the drifts melted and the days grew longer, we knew it was the time to fix fence. Some of it would have to be done before we brought our horses up from their winter pasture in the low country. So with backpacks loaded with tools, splicing wire and staples, we went on our way to start repairs on drift and boundary fences below us.

Mary always looked forward to this day with the excitement of a girl headed for a school picnic. She liked to fix fence. She said it made her feel like she was getting something done.

Above our heads, in a clear azure sky, a pair of red-tailed hawks soared in widening circles. Mary looked up. Through squinted eyes, she watched the two. She was pleased. "I'm glad our neighbors are coming back," she said. "I hope we see the kestrels, too."

The fall of the land below our cabin was sharp. As we descended the steep sides of Powderhorn Canyon, the difference in plant growth was noticeable. I read somewhere that for every two-hundred-foot loss in elevation, the climatic change is about the same as going south seventy-two miles.

Because she is a botanist at heart, Mary was more alert to the changes than I. To Mary, a plant noticed for the first time in any new season is an important discovery. Even if the plant is only up a couple inches, it draws her interest.

She bent down to examine the new growth closely. "See here, Mark," she said. "See how that leaf unfolds. You'll be able to identify this one next time, won't you?"

I nodded. I always nod. But I think I do well to know some of them when the blossoms are out big and pretty.

 Tasha, a young German shepherd who had joined our family the fall before, and Skipper had come along with us. They were having a fine time digging down into the moist, soft earth for gophers and mice.

On short switchback courses across the open slope, we dropped deeper into the canyon. Surely there was a climatic change. We opened our jackets and shifted the straps on our backpacks.

As we continued down, a small herd of elk and a couple of bunches of mule deer moved farther up on hillsides and watched us go by. Along our path, we saw an early elk calf lying still as a stone, close to a clump of sage. Both dogs sniffed at the rump of the calf and trotted on. The infant elk never blinked an eye.

Up on the hillsides, the elk had returned their attention to seeking out the still-folded leaves of balsam root and the new green grass along with the dry, brown feed remaining from the year before.

By the time we reached the lower drift fence, we had lost two thousand feet in elevation. Snowdrifts and chill winds were a long way behind us.

Here the range grass was a healthy, dark green and was up six inches or so. On the green slopes, lupine and larkspur showed up as light and dark blue. Dandelions made yellow patches here and there.

From deeper in the canyon, we heard the roar of the Powderhorn, wild in its plunge to the low country. The sheer rock wall on the other side did its part to turn the sound our way.

That whole, big, awesome gash in the side of the mountain had the power of a magnet. It drew a man's eye, and ear, and mind. But this day we had short time to be mesmerized. We came to fix fence, and that we must do.

Working up the slope toward home, we started on the job. We spliced broken wires and replaced missing staples. When the wires were slack, we tightened whole sections.

The morning passed quickly. Through the years, we had come to like a special place where we ate our lunch. There, a leaning rock as big as a small barn faced the south. The sun beat in and warmed the sandy floor of the shelter. Close by, a tiny stream babbled on its way.

As we munched on sandwiches, we were rewarded with a rare treat—the spirit-lifting song of a meadowlark. We seldom saw that happy bird this high. On a little rise nearby, a blue grouse strutted, his tail fanned out, low booming sounds coming from the air sacs in his neck.

Behind us rose a rimrock a few hundred feet high and well over a mile long. Along its face, cliff swallows made their home. They are busy birds, wheeling and darting, landing and taking flight. Since we had worked fence at this place last year, the swallows had made their winter migration to Central America, or maybe a bit farther, and then had returned to this very place.

Aloud, Mary and I wondered what makes these swallows migrate specifically to Central America. Surely the mosquitos and flies in Louisiana and coastal Texas must be as tasty as those in Honduras. And why do they return on schedule, year after year, to this particular rimrock, in this particular range within the vast Rocky Mountain chain?

We mused on that subject for awhile. Then we concluded that what was really important to us was that we could have confidence that next year the swallows would be wheeling and darting along this very same rimrock, just as they were now.

But with fence to fix, we couldn't muse too long on any subject. Most years it took us two or three days to reach the end of that fence at eight-thousand feet. We shouldered our packs and moved along to access the winter's damage.

Both heavy snow in deep drifts and the normal traffic of animals do their part to wreck a fence. Elk and deer have no respect for drift and boundary fences. To them it's all one mountain, and it all belongs to them. Deer, at times, go under the bottom wire if enough space is there. Elk calves go between the strands. Mature elk almost always go over the top. Clearing a six-foot obstacle is no problem for an elk. But I think sometimes they are of a rather lazy mind. They jump no higher than necessary to get to the other side. Often as they go over, they hit a wire. They break it or stretch it and pull staples free of wooden posts up and down the line.

Then, too, a neighbor's bull has been known to want to get to the other side where the grass is greener or the cows more receptive or, often, for no good reason at all.

That day as we worked along the fence, I got to thinking about our neighbor, Lilly Dundee, and her infamous white bull. Actually, the bull is not white. He is a Hereford, but he is liberally splashed with white. I always refer to him as Lilly's white bull.

Lilly ranches down in the low country on land her father homesteaded about a century ago. Lilly is a widow, and, respectfully, I reveal that she has seen eighty summers and winters. With some hired help, Lilly does a good job of getting the cows bred on time and calved out with a minimal loss. She gets the hay up in good shape and never runs short.

Summed up, I like Lilly. She is a fine person. And a good neighbor, too. Except for one thing. She owns the white bull.

Lilly summers her cattle a few miles from here in a pasture which adjoins the summer range of our cattle. That's where the trouble started with the white bull.

The white bull has a little age on him. He is wise to the ways of cows, and he stays home until his job is done.

One day last summer I rode down that way. Lilly's cows behaved like cows do when they know they are going to have another calf come spring. On a knoll, off to the side, stood the white bull. He chewed his cud and looked over the fence. I was proud of the fence. It was stretched up tight and all the staples were in. I looked at the bull, and I started getting mad. But I guess you can't arrest a man or a bull for just looking over a fence. I rode on without looking back.

Sure enough, the next time I rode down that way, the white bull was on the wrong side of the fence. He wasn't very far inside our pasture, and he stood on a knoll, chewing

Victoria 1991

his cud and looking back over the fence at Lilly's cows. The fence had a big hole in it where he had broken wires and pulled the staples. The way was wide open for the bull to go home, but he wouldn't do it.

Not very gently, I took the bull home to his own cows and repaired the fence. That went on all summer. It got to the point that just riding down that way and thinking about the white bull gave me a bellyache.

That fall, I rode along the county road near Lilly's place. I had taken down a few head of cattle that had been missed in the roundup, and I was on the way home. I stopped to see Lilly.

Lilly always greeted me warmly.

"Lilly," I said, "I've come to see about the white bull again."

"Sit down, Mark," Lilly said, "have a cup of coffee." She poured a steaming cup.

"Now, Lilly, about that bull," I tried again.

"Have some cake, Mark. I know you like chocolate." Lilly put a big piece in front of me.

I dug in and took a bigger-than-I-should forkful. That was a mistake. With my mouth full, I couldn't talk. Already, Lilly had me at a disadvantage. As I finished up my cake, I planned my attack. I wasn't smiling now.

"Lilly, you've got to get rid of that bull."

Lilly put on her sweetest little-old-lady face. "What bull, Mark?"

On my lap, I clenched my fists so hard my knuckles turned white. "What bull! You know darn right well what bull. It's that son-of-a-gun of a fence-crawling white bull that wears your brand on his side." I regretted immediately that I had shouted at Lilly.

Lilly showed concern. "Oh, Mark, did he get in a fight and cripple one of your bulls?"

"No."

"Did any of your cows have calves last spring that were marked like my bull?"

"No."

Lilly's lips firmed up. "Well, what's all the fuss about? He can't eat much of your grass. His teeth are about gone, and his feet are bad."

I put my head down and counted to ten before I answered. "It isn't how much he eats. It's just that he keeps going back and forth, and he makes a new gate every time he does. Look, Lilly, why don't you sell him for bologna and buy a new range bull?" I was sorry I had waved my arms so much.

By then Lilly's chin had jutted out a notch, and we both were standing up.

"Sell him!" Lilly spat out the words. "The way the market is now? I'm not going to do it." Lilly looked me straight in the eye, her arms folded across her chest.

I blew through my lips and searched for words.

Then right before my eyes, Lilly's face became transformed. She looked up at me with saintly benevolence. From a chair close by, she took a half-filled grain sack. "Here, Mark, take these home. It's just some beets and carrots. I pulled them this morning after I saw you go by with those cows. I thought you might stop by."

I didn't know what to say.

Lilly opened the door. "God bless you, Mark. Have a safe ride up the mountain. Give my love to Mary."

I sort of staggered out, and Lilly closed the door behind me. Going off the porch, I swear I heard Lilly chuckle.

ø ø ø

A whole winter had passed since that encounter. Here on the mountain, I looked around and took in the beautiful spring day. Then I drove a staple in a pine post and tried not to think of another summer with Lilly's white bull.

 Horses & Saddles

W ITH A LIGHT PACK on my back, I swung along in a
ground-eating stride, enjoying the sights and sounds
and smells of an awakening mountainside. I had been
restless the past week or so; anxious to get our horses back up
on the mountain, so I could start making fresh tracks into
country I hadn't seen since the fall before. Now that we had
good grass at our elevation, I didn't have to delay any longer.
Headed for the low country, I could hardly wait to get there.
When I came back up, I would be a man on a horse again.

Hidden from the sun because of the lay of the land, the
snowdrifts that build up on the Gunshot Trail linger until the
new season is well advanced. I walked at the outer edge of the
track where the depth of the slanting drifts was the least.

Although I lost altitude rapidly, travel conditions hardly
changed until I reached the viewpoint of Last Chance Rock.
From there, the country below looked especially green and
summer-like. Warm air wafted up from the meadows and
foothills and gave my cheeks a pleasant caress.

I lifted my binoculars to my eyes and searched the draws
and flats for our horses. At the rim of Ponderosa Canyon, I
saw the bunch. They had already been down to the creek for
water and had gone back up on top to graze.

Continuing on down, I lengthened and quickened my
stride. I wanted to catch up with the horses before they

decided to make a run to the far parts of the foothill range. I slowed down only once. That was to examine the fresh prints of a mountain lion in the moist earth. As always, the sight of the tracks stirred me.

I made catch-up steps following the switchback trail down into the canyon. In the bottom, I rock-hopped across the creek and climbed to the rim on the south side.

The horses had moved off some distance, but they caught sight of me as I came out on the open flat. They threw up their heads and faced my way. It had probably been a while since they had last seen a rider, to say nothing of a man afoot.

The horses swapped ends. Tails aloft, they started to quit the country. Cupping my hands to my mouth, I called to them as I had done many times before. The bunch slowed down. Turning my way again, they stopped in their tracks, heads up, ears pricked forward. I called again. A few hesitating steps at a time, they came closer. I talked to them now, coaxingly. One horse nickered. Then another. At once, they danced a zigzag course to meet me.

I barely had time to slip off my pack to remove the grain cake and halter I had brought with me. Shoving and pushing, the horses crowded around me, each trying to be the first to get a handout of the feed. It had been a long time since they had enjoyed the taste of grain.

I thought the horses looked good, hair slicked off and about as fat as they ought to be. Most of them had picked up a few burrs during the winter, but it wouldn't take long to clean them up.

My inspection over, I haltered the first handy horse and led him off. The rest of the bunch followed. Then, one by one, they dropped behind to graze. My wrangling horse turned once and nickered to his herd mates. I spoke sharply and gave a light tug to his lead rope, and he came along. I still had a few miles to go before I would drop down on Deer Creek. From there I would phone our horseshoer.

Anvil and I always have to find out how the other has wintered. Through the years, I've found that horseshoers are a good source of ranch country news. I made the most of that. Then we got down to business.

On the day we had set for the shoeing, I rode out and wrangled the rest of the string. Later, with the horses shod, I considered the summer season started.

ø ø ø

Most years when I went down for the horses, I didn't waste much time in the low country, but it still took a few days to get everything done. That spring, my trip was typical. We had two grain sacks of mail waiting for us. Half of it was Christmas greetings we would have enjoyed in December, but would still be able to enjoy in June. There were phone calls to make and people to see. And, of course, there was shopping to do.

I tried to get turned around and headed back as soon as I could. Mary worried about me when I was off down the mountain. She was concerned I might get run over crossing the streets in town or smash up our pickup. It reached the point where I practically had to take a driver's license test before she'd give me the car keys.

She told me, "Why, I would just as soon see you ride up Doomsday Creek during a lightning storm on a horse that bucks than turn you loose in that town by yourself."

Anyhow, one morning I was ready so I wrangled my horses before daylight, then grained and saddled them. As the horses were soft from loafing all winter, I packed them light.

It was a happy moment when I rode through the gate on the way back to the high country. I enjoyed the feel of the springy step of the horse I rode. Behind me, I led as good a

string of pack horses as any man ever took to the mountains.

Much later that day when I pulled into our camp, Mary and the dogs gave me a warm welcome. Our cat acted as though she never knew I was gone.

After supper, we had a grand time reading the Christmas messages from people close and far away. By the time we got the packages opened, the room looked like a disaster area. We talked until late. There was six months' news to catch up on.

ø ø ø

Each spring, there came a day when Mary felt compelled to go down off the mountain herself. I never saw signs of eager anticipation written on her face.

I remember the occasion one year. The first faint streaks of dawn were showing in the east when Mary stepped into the saddle. She rode Topper, her favorite. Behind, she led Kyska and Quito packing empty panniers.

I walked ahead and opened the gate as she came my way. Mary looked glum. "Go to town. Go to town. That's all I seem to do. Why I just got back from town last fall."

"Maybe you'll like it."

Mary gave me a dirty look. Then quickly her eyes crinkled into mischief lines I know well.

"Honey, if that Sacajawea woman comes by, you be sure to tell her to keep on going. Mark, are you listening to me?"

"No."

Mary laughed and blew me a kiss as she rode through the gate, sitting tall and straight in the saddle.

She wasn't very far along the trail when I called after her. "Don't forget to tighten up the britchen on those pack horses before you start down that steep place."

Mary didn't even turn around. She shook her head and pointed her nose in the air. That was her way of telling me she knew what to do about those pack horses.

I closed the gate and strode slowly back toward the cabin half-hidden among the trees. I stopped and looked. I liked what I saw. The logs had been stained as dark as the trunks of the Englemann spruce and lodgepole pine around it. On the roof, the shakes had curled out of shape and weathered to a dark gray. White smoke from the damped-off stove lifted in a lazy swirl above the ridge. The cabin looked as though it had been there a long time. As though it belonged to the mountain—a part of the land on which it lay. I thought if I was going to be a bachelor for a while, this was a pretty good place to batch.

Almost a week later, I was working at the bench of our outdoor saddle shop doing some repair work that I really should have done the fall before. Both dogs were stretched out dozing in the late afternoon sun. At once, they raised their heads and listened. I listened too. From along the trail I heard a whistled tune. Without barking, the dogs took off like a flash. I walked over and opened the gate.

From a distance, Mary waved gaily. As usual her horses were packed just as they should be: loads evenly balanced, the green cover tarps the same length on each side, and the double diamonds pictures of perfection.

The dogs made an awful fuss, whining and jumping around and wiggling all over. I was more reserved, but I allowed that if I was going to be a hermit, I'd just as soon have Mary around to help me be one.

Green Moon

T HE UNPREDICTABLE DAYS of late spring were left
behind, and the generous days of early summer moved
in. By that time, Mary and I had boundary and drift
fences in order. We'd opened or closed gates, depending on
how the cattle were to be managed during the early part of
the grazing season.

Ranges that had been grazed early the year before would
be rested until the late summer. Grass and other range plants
would be allowed to grow up tall and strong. In doing so, the
plants would make their own food. Some of it would be used
for normal growth and to make fertile seed. A part of it would
be stored in the roots and stem bases of the plant. That reserve
would supply nourishment to the plant during the winter and
would start growth the next spring.

ø ø ø

Packing out salt to strategic locations before the cattle
arrive on this high country scene is usually a pleasant chore. It
seemed especially so one year I have in mind.

We had received early rains and the moisture brought
up the grass nicely. Now, it seemed, those sun-hungry plants
reached up another inch or so each day. The outlook for good
feed was promising, not only for the cattle, but for the elk
and deer as well.

So early one morning I rode off for the salt cache with

three pack horses in tow. Tasha, our German shepherd, trotted just ahead of my saddle horse. Skipper stayed home nursing a bandaged front foot that had been cut by a sharp chip of rock on the trail.

Mary was home, too. About this time of year, she usually had a good time fussing about in her miniature garden. She did fine on the mountain with root crops and things like lettuce and spinach. One year Mary wanted to put in a crop of potatoes. I fenced off a place with poles to keep the horses out. Mary irrigated and hoed the plants that came up. But the growing season is short up in the high country. She got some potatoes that fall, but not enough to glut the market.

I tried to manage my work in such a way that in the late summer, I packed up the mountain all the salt that I would need the next year. In that way, if we got late spring snows and the trails became clogged, I wouldn't find myself on top without salt for the cattle. Someone from the ranch or the cattle association trucked the salt to the bottom of the trail. Thereafter, whenever I had a chance, I went down with three or four pack horses and moved it up the mountain. On those days, I got moving as soon as it was light enough to see to catch a horse. That allowed me time to get down and load the packhorses with salt before those lower-country flies drove my horses to distraction. With that schedule, I also hoped to beat late afternoon electric storms. I've never found it comforting to be caught leading a string of pack horses up a canyon with the thunder and lightning cracking and flashing around me.

So that morning, I pulled up in front of the salt cabin with my string, ready to load salt I had packed up the year before. In front of the cabin, in early summer, white clover grew thick and lush. My horses lowered their heads and started to feed. There was no need to tie them up. I picked up the lead rope of my number one horse in the string and tied him near the door of the storage cabin. Hanging on each side of the packsaddle, by a loop of rope around the crossbucks, was an open box. We call them salt panniers. Each pannier will carry two fifty-pound blocks of salt.

The panniers are, of necessity, of rugged construction to stand up under the wear and tear of carrying block salt. I make mine out of three-quarter-inch plywood, reinforced with angle iron. The inside measurements of the bottoms are about nine-by-twenty inches. That holds the salt snug enough, but allows sufficient space so a man won't smash his fingers as he handles the blocks—he hopes.

As soon as two blocks of salt were loaded on each side, I took an old horseshoer's rasp and rounded off the sharp edges of the blocks. Now when I snugged up my double diamond hitch, my lash rope wouldn't get cut as it passed over the edges of the salt block. I packed each horse the same way. The horses were reluctant to leave the clover, but nevertheless, off we went to get our salt out on the range.

The high country air was still brisk, and the horses moved out with eager steps. From the top of a dead lodgepole, a flycatcher called out in loud, clear notes. I had to smile. It seemed the bird was saying, "Quick, three beers!"

As we passed through Shonto Park, brown and tan rockchucks scurried through the grass as we approached. Their trails were well-worn by repeated trips to the creek for water. Now they disappeared underground, below big rocks here and there. But not all of them, I learned. From atop a tall outcropping of granite, a sentinel whistled a warning to others of his kind farther down the creek.

Leaving the park, we crossed a creek where smaller than pan-sized trout wiggled and splashed in the shallow water. We climbed a sagebrush slope and went over a divide into a steep aspen-fringed draw where timothy already grew rank along some seep springs. With haunches close to the ground, the horses picked their way to the bottom. There, I gave wide berth to a swamp where I had gotten in a jackpot before.

So it went that morning. Working from one grassy park to another, I dropped off two blocks at a time. As far as the nutritional needs of cattle were concerned, most summer range provides the salt cattle need. But, by making salt readily available, a stockman insures that their needs are actually met. Most of all, salt is a tool used to get proper distribution of cattle on the range. Early in life, they acquire a taste for the stuff, and they will walk a considerable distance to get some.

Most stockmen using high country grass feel it is good management to take small bunches of cattle to many parts of the range. Usually cattle are the most content when they are not crowded by other bovine critters. And certainly, the range itself does the best when it is not too crowded by cattle. There seems to be some evidence that elk and deer like this arrangement, too, probably because they are less likely to feel their summer domain is being invaded.

I put out the last two blocks of salt on lower Marten Creek, so named because one time in the fall I had seen a pine marten there, bounding along the backbones of some deadfalls. Marten Creek Park is a nice place to eat lunch. The park consists of about sixty acres of dry grassland sloping down to the creek. At the top of the slope, gray crags stand tall as watchtowers over the remote place. Across the creek, pine and spruce reach back through some rough up-and-down country. Marten Creek Park doesn't offer much as far as a grand vista is concerned, but it is a quiet place, seemingly cut off from the rest of the world.

I slacked the cinch on Nugget, my saddle horse, then untied my pack horses one from the other and let them all

graze. From my saddlebag, I removed the lunch Mary had put
there. Then I found a sun-warmed
rock that sloped just right for me to
lean back and watch white, feathery
clouds sail across a blue sky. Tasha
lay close by and listened with half-
interest to the chatter of a squirrel across the creek.

o o o

Tasha is really Mary's dog. She only comes with me on
special occasions. How well I remember the day Tasha
joined our family. She was a Christmas present to Mary from
some very good friends.

Tasha arrived at Deer Creek in one of those plastic carriers the airlines refer to as sky kennels. She was a weanling
puppy, all black at that time, and she was whimpering. It was
the day before Thanksgiving, and it was twenty below zero.
Obviously, the puppy couldn't climb the mountain on her
own. Like just about everything that came to our camp, she
traveled by pack horse. I picked Nugget for the job.

I loaded the sky kennel on Nugget's left side and covered it with a down sleeping bag I brought along for the purpose. Mail went on the other side to balance the load. I placed
a tarp over the top and lashed the whole caboodle snug with a
double diamond. Then we made tracks for the high country
through six inches of fresh snow.

The puppy never whimpered as we climbed the steep
trail. I couldn't see her back there under the tarp. I wished
she would bark, or cry, or do whatever puppies are supposed
to do. Mary was looking forward to the arrival of the puppy.
I didn't want anything to happen to it. Even in that cold temperature, Nugget had worked up some heat scratching up that
slippery trail. Certainly, I thought, some of the warmth from

the horse should get through to help keep the puppy warm.

Anyhow, we made the trip in good shape. I was relieved to be able to carry the sky kennel and its cargo into the warm cabin. When we opened the door of the kennel, the black German shepherd puppy tottered out and looked around with big, brown eyes. They came to rest on Mary. She picked up the puppy and cradled it in her arms. The puppy whimpered quietly, then tried to lick Mary's face. Tasha had found her special person. It has been that way ever since.

◊ ◊ ◊

My lunch finished, I lay back against my sloping rock and surveyed the scene through half-closed eyes. The three sorrels, Kyska, Travis, and Happy Jack, grazed side by side. Nugget, the leggy brown, is sort of a pestiferous horse, not at all popular with his herd mates. Today, he thought it wise to keep his distance.

From over a timbered ridge, a golden eagle came our way in a shallow glide. The big bird of prey flew so low I could see him move his head from side to side. Over a stretch of rimrock, he picked up a midday thermal. The eagle flapped his wings a few times. Then soaring, he rode the air current, rising with easy grace from one level to another. I watched the eagle travel in ever widening circles until my eyes watered and I lost him against the pale-blue sky and bright sun.

Reflecting back on the morning and further back through the years, I felt a warm contentment. Life had been good to me. I found good reason to love life. And, it seemed the more I loved life, the more it loved me back. I looked forward to each new day with pleasant anticipation.

Tomorrow would see me packing salt into the Agate Creek Country, a place several miles from where I now rested. By mid-afternoon, I should have all the salt out on the range that the cattle would need for the early part of the summer.

The Agate Creek Country is one of my favorite places. Anytime I top out on the divide overlooking Agate Creek, I feel compelled to pull up my horse and let my eyes feast on the scene below. What we refer to as Agate Creek Country is really a valley about four miles long. The south slope is forested, and it stretches a long way back through some rough terrain. The north slope is open grassland, reaching from the creek to the base of Little Baldy and Big Baldy, two small, rock-topped mountains that overlook the valley. Down through the bottom on a westerly course, Agate Creek flows in a series of horseshoe bends.

I remember well the day I went in there to salt that country one year. The valley at that time had a clean, untouched look with the land freshly washed by melting snow and early rains. The grass had a good start, and on that carpet of green, the blue of lupine and pasque flowers showed in a grand array.

At that time of year, the elk gather into herds sometimes numbering as many as two hundred head of cows, calves, and young bulls. As I rode over the divide, I saw them spread out grazing on the early grass, testing the immature leaves of currant bushes and occasionally nipping off the yellow head of a dandelion.

Since the morning was well on, some of the elk were lying down, soaking up the sun. Some of the calves nosed their mothers, trying for another gulp of milk. A few frisked about with others of their kind.

A wise old cow was the first to be alerted by my progress down the valley. She stood, head up, her big ears forward, looking in my direction. With her nose moving from side to side, her inquisitive nostrils searched the breeze that came her way. Soon other cows stopped their grazing and looked my way. A few that were lying down got to their feet. First one, then two or three, shifted nervously. With noses elevated, they

trotted a weaving course through the fringe of the herd.

More heads came up. Nervous tension spread. Now the entire herd became alerted. A young bull barked in alarm. A cow with her calf trotted down the slope. Another pair followed. As if on signal, cows, calves and bulls burst into a breakneck gallop. Drumming hooves drove them on. Now stampeding, they hurtled dry washes and clumps of sage. Calves only a few weeks old stretched out close in the wake of their mothers. At the lip of the creek bank, they soared. One after the other they landed in midstream, and water splashed high in the air. In a couple of noisy minutes the herd had crossed the creek and disappeared into the timber on the far side.

Now bedlam erupted. Cows and calves that had become separated in flight searched for each other in a vocal way. Calves gave out with high-pitched squeals. Cows replied in much the same way, only louder and the tone more mature.

From my position high up on the slope, I could see into the small openings in the forest.

The herd slowed down. Some stopped to graze. Little by little, cows and calves found each other and moved along together. The noise sounded less frantic. More calves bleated instead of squealing. After awhile, I heard just the normal cow-calf talk of a slowly moving band.

I continued to ride toward the west, staying high up on the grassy slope, well away from the creek. I dropped off salt, two or four blocks at a time, at places the cattle knew well. The elk would eat some of that salt before the big herd broke up and scattered to the far reaches of the range.

With the last of the salt dumped off, I turned and headed for camp. Glad to be free of their loads, the pack horses danced about. The lead horse got nipped on the rump. Another reached down and grabbed a mouthful of grass on the go.

Activity well below us caught their eyes, and four sets of ears pointed that way.

Down in the bottom, I saw the same herd of elk that had stampeded a couple of hours before. They were strung out along the creek, some grazing, others loafing. Many had their nostrils dipped to the cold, clear water taking on an afternoon fill. A couple pawed in the creek with front hooves, splashing water over their backs. Up and down a gravel bar, two cows played, shaking their heads and running in crazy circles. A half-dozen calves looked on as interested spectators. Many of the elk had become alerted by our passing high above them. Some trotted to and fro nervously. A few moved into the timber then came back out at once.

I rode on, looking back over my shoulder. Down on the creek, the elk had settled down, some feeding, others lying down to chew their cuds. I was tempted to stop and watch the more tranquil behavior of the herd. I thought again. On that bright day, I truly felt the Valley of the Agate was more their home than mine.

ø ø ø

That's the way it had been one year when I put out salt on Agate Creek. I wondered what I would find when I went into Agate Creek Country the next day.

Barney

WHEN PACKSADDLES GET used as much as Mary and I use them, something is bound to wear out. We knew that it was a wise move to go over the outfits periodically. By doing so, we might be able to replace a worn cinch or strap before it broke. When pack gear breaks on the trail, it usually spells trouble for man or horse or both.

One afternoon I worked in the shade of a tall Engelmann spruce, handling a saddle that had given us lots of service over the years. I had modified the tree of the saddle so it fit the back of a pack horse I had used long ago. For sure, the horse wasn't the best I ever packed. But for many reasons, he was a horse I will always remember with good feeling. His name was Barney.

Barney was a black Percheron. He was range raised, so he didn't get as big as his breeding would have allowed. Barney pushed the scale down to thirteen-fifty when he was in good working shape.

Barney was low-withered. He had to be packed just right. If not, a man might find the saddle and load had slipped off to the side. Worse yet, the careless packer might find the whole caboodle under the horse's belly. Most horses would consider that situation to be cause enough for an insurrection. Not Barney. He always stood patiently while the mess was untangled and made right.

Barney had a weak point or two, but he was strong on personality. Any man who used the black gelding liked him. If pressed for a reason, the hand might shrug his shoulders and say, "Oh, I don't know. He is just kind of nice to be around."

Big as he was, Barney was as sensitive as a child. I can remember only a couple of times that I thought he needed to be scolded. When I did, Barney's lower lip would tremble, and he would turn his head away as if he were going to cry.

Barney came to the ranch in some kind of horse trade. He was just a colt then. That was before I arrived on the scene. Once I talked to an old hand who told me the cowboys used to try to ride Barney bareback. Nobody could stay on for more than a couple of jumps.

By the time I caught up with Barney, he had been used as a pack horse for several years. Someplace along the line, Barney must have gotten in a tight squeeze with a pack. Going along a trail, I never knew him to scrape a pack on a tree. He approached each tree with suspicion. He snorted, cocked his head, and then danced around the tree in a wide half-circle.

Barney felt the same way about going through a barn door. He always gave the same exhibition. He stopped and rolled his eyes. Then, snorting, he charged through the middle. A man had to step lively to keep from getting spread on the barn floor.

One year at Deer Creek, we needed a replacement in a winter feed team. I broke Barney to drive and put him to work with a Clydesdale named Jack. They matched up well and made a good team.

Barney's behavior pattern was the same each midday. We usually got back from feeding the cows on the meadow just before noon. Then we grained the team in the barn and pulled off their harnesses. Next we curried the horses and turned them loose in the corral. Each day Jack went out first, slow and steady-like. Barney dashed through the doorway as if the devil had a hold on his tail. Outside, Barney shook his head and looked back to where he had just come from. That done, he laid down and rolled—once, twice, three times. As soon as he got to his feet, he started bucking. His head down between his front legs, snorting and grunting, without fail Barney bucked his way to the creek in jolting, stiff-legged jumps. There, the black horse took a long, unhurried drink. Turning, he nonchalantly ambled over to the hay bunk and started nibbling on the good grass hay.

The next summer, Alkali Rob packed Barney whenever he went up to the cow camp. Among other things, Rob took care of the brood mares and rode the colts for the ranch. He was a top hand and still is.

At the time, I rode a gray four-year-old named Biscuit. I liked him. He had enough thoroughbred in him to have a good set of withers and plenty of daylight under his belly. But at times, he was more horse than I wanted. Rob noticed it and suggested that he take Biscuit to the mountains and use him for a while. I agreed.

Rob took Barney and Biscuit along with some other horses to the high country. At the cow camp, a relationship developed that surprised Rob.

Barney had always been pretty cranky with most other horses. He preferred that they keep their distance—especially when he was eating. But up there, Barney took a shine to Biscuit. In fact, he took the young gray under his wing like an old mother hen. Heads down in a patch of clover, the two would have their muzzles so close that you might think they were yoked together. If another horse came close, Barney lifted his head and put his ears back. That was all it took to discourage the intruder.

One evening after supper, Rob looked out across the

pasture just in time to see an unrehearsed drama enacted.

Biscuit was showing a streak of independence by grazing some distance away from Barney. He was nipping off some choice grass on the west side of the pasture where the fence ran along a stand of lodgepole pine. Biscuit was so busy trying to fill his belly that he didn't see the big black bear coming out of the forest. The bear clambered over the pole fence not far from where Biscuit was grazing.

The bear looked neither to the left nor to the right. He traveled as though he owned the whole mountain, including the horse pasture. He moved with a steady determination that said it was going to take more than a half-dozen horses to keep him from crossing there.

At length, Biscuit did look up—and he saw the bear. The colt whinnied in fright. Swapping ends, he raced back to dance nervously at Barney's side.

The black horse was already alert. He stood foursquare, head up, ears forward, eyeing the bear.

The bear kept coming.

Barney trotted forward a dozen yards and stopped.

The bear stopped, too.

Barney pawed sand from a gopher mound up over his shoulder, like a challenging range bull.

The bear, nearsighted like all his kind, stood up on his hind legs for a better look. He pawed the air and champed his teeth.

Behind Barney, Biscuit whinnied nervously and moved about.

The bear came down on all fours.

At once, Barney squealed like a fighting stallion. With ears pinned back and his yellowed teeth bared viciously, he drove himself toward the bear.

The bear gave one woof and turned tail. In his haste to

get away, his sharp-clawed feet made the sod fly. With surprising speed for an animal of such bulk, the bear closed the gap between danger and safety. A pine pole snapped and splintered as the bruin went through the fence in a manner more bull-like than bear-like.

Barney stopped at the pole fence. In a moment, Biscuit was at his side. The old black horse's nostrils flared and his eyes flashed as he and the young gray horse watched the retreating bear disappear into the darkening forest.

 Fresh Range

A CHANGE COMES UPON the high country during the last days of June. That is when herds belonging to local ranchers arrive on the summer range.

Each cattle association using the different ranges selects its own range boss from among its members. The range boss is the coordinator between the administrator of the rented grass pasture and the ranchers. He is also the person with whom the rider for the association does most of his business.

There comes a day when it is apparent the grass is ready in the high country. The word gets around.

Each rancher is responsible for getting his own cattle to the summer range. Neighbors talk it over as to which herd will start up on what day. In that way, there is little chance that a bovine traffic jam will occur.

Herds are shaped up before the drive. An old cow crippled with a stifled left hindquarter is cut away with her calf. Another cow with a newborn calf is sorted the same way. A bull turns up lame and has to be replaced. They could never keep up with the herd on the long drive up the mountain.

Each outfit has wise old cows that have summered on the mountain since they were calves at the side of other wise old cows. As June moves toward a close, they get restless on those low-country meadows. The days get hotter, the flies get thicker, and usually the grass gets shorter. A rider with the observing eye of a stockman will notice those mountain-wise cows gazing longingly toward the far ridges or feeding closer to the gate than has been their habit. They are ready to head up those dusty county roads and lead the rest of the herd toward the foot of the mountain.

For the riders who push cattle to the summer range, it is a time of saddling up before daylight, sniffing trail dust all day, and pulling a saddle off about sundown. They are often thirsty and sometimes a bit hungry. But it is a social time, too. The ranchers who bring cattle up to the mountain operate family-type ventures. Women and children get mounted as well as the men, and most likely, a few family friends saddle up, too. I can remember certain youngsters riding up behind a herd years ago. They still push cattle up the mountain, only now they have their own kids riding alongside to help.

Ranchers and their riders camp at the foot of the mountain the night before they start the cattle up the steep, rocky trail. Supper might be late, but there is always enough of it. After awhile, big people and little people crawl into bedrolls for a short night. Their herds graze nearby for a time, then cows and calves and bulls bed down. The cattle chew their cuds, belch loudly once in awhile, but mostly rest.

To the riders it seems like the middle of the night when they are roused out. Breakfast is eaten around the fire in the chill pre-dawn air. Then the horses are caught and saddled.

A few cows and calves stand around. Some calves nurse. Most pairs are still bedded down side by side. A couple of riders, who were the first to saddle up, ride through the herd getting cows and calves to their feet. Soon hungry bovine youngsters start their breakfasts. At nursing time, calves don't have dainty manners. They butt with their heads, slurp loudly, and white milk foam runs down their chins. But they do get their fill.

After awhile, a veteran cow of many trips to the mountain points her nose at the foot of the trail and moves that way. Her calf stands and watches her go for a moment or so, then follows in her wake.

More riders get mounted and give out with a whoop and a holler to let the herd know it is time to move out. Cows and calves talk back and forth. By ones and twos, they fall in behind the pair that took the lead. Soon a sea of bobbing heads is moving toward the foot of the trail.

A top hand rides at the point and nudges the leaders over a notch or two, and they hit the trail just right. The riders in the drag hold back a bit to let the cattle string out. The swing and flank riders move along at the side of the herd. Before very long, the cattle move up the trail in a long, thin line.

At the drag, a few extra calves collect, those that did not keep up with their mothers. Up ahead a cow turns around, bawls for her calf, and blocks the trail as she does. A calf cuts back for the bedground as that is where he thinks his mother is. It takes some wild riding on the side of a hill to get the calf turned and pushed back to the herd. And always, it seems, there is a bull who would rather be off the trail than on it. But, in general, all goes pretty well as the herd, encouraged on by the chant of the riders, sidles up the steep side of the canyon. One well-earned step at a time, the cattle move away from the low country with its face flies and hot weather toward a fresh range for the summer.

Up on top, I meet up with cow people and cows. I've known these ranchers for years. They are a breed of their own. I'm proud to call them friends. Riding along, I visit with this one and that.

I haven't seen most of these people since the cattle went off the mountain the previous fall. Whatever else we talk about, I'm sure to be asked these questions:

"How did you winter, Mark?"

"How's Mary?"

"How's the grass, Mark?"

It has been said that cattle ranching is one of the last frontiers of individualism. A valid statement, I think. Most of the cowmen I know wouldn't trade their independence for an easier, more financially rewarding job in town. They like the smell of horse sweat, cows and green grass. It might be hard to get one to admit it, but they get a lift from seeing an orange sun-ball flooding an eastern sky and hearing the meadowlark music that accompanies the scene.

A cowman has no patience with the thought of being shackled by union rules. And he feels that too many government regulations are a shackle, too.

Quietly, he enjoys the memory of a walk shared with his wife, of going down to the calving barn to see that all was well in the night. And long after it has happened, the same cowman is still warmed by the pride he felt to have a son or daughter riding stirrup to stirrup with him on a ride through the herd.

Worrying about the mortgage held at the bank has probably done as much to add gray hairs to his head as has long, hard days afoot or on horseback. The cowman cusses the weather when it doesn't fit with his plans. And he cusses the uncertainty of the cattle market. But when the chips are down, he shrugs his shoulders and meets the risks of each day as they come.

The cattle that come up the mountain nowadays look a bit different than they did in years past. They used to be all Herefords; but now as a herd strings out, you can pick any color you want. Crossbreeding to get the best traits of two breeds seems to be the way many stockmen are going.

The cattle from each ranch are trailed to their allotted

place on the range. From that time on, I do the moving of the cattle to meet the needs of cow and range.

As much as those ranch folks would like to stay, they don't linger long on the mountain. Down in the lower country, there is never a shortage of work to do. They have irrigating to do and hay to be put up for winter feed. That goes on all summer and into early fall.

Usually these good neighbors of ours do take time to stop by and visit with Mary for a spell. Then with a wave of a hand and a pleasant farewell, they ride on down the trail. We won't see them again until the cattle are gathered in the fall.

Maggie

CAPUCHIN, THE BLACK and white kitten that came up the mountain on a pack mule that first fall, grew into a nice cat. She was a good mouser, and she was Tasha's special friend. Capuchin slept snuggled up to Tasha's flank, and the dog seemed glad to have her there.

It was obvious that Capuchin liked Mary and me. As far as people were concerned that is where it started and stopped. Whenever a visitor rode into camp, Capuchin disappeared. Hours after the strange voice was no longer heard, the cat would come back to join the family.

Our grandchildren came up for a visit and stayed a few days. They were toddlers at the time, and they had the exuberance of youngsters of that age. Capuchin fled at the first sound of their excited voices. For days after the children left, Mary searched and called for the cat. By the law of the wild, Capuchin was fair prey for coyote or bobcat or owl or eagle or hawk. We never saw Capuchin again.

A few weeks later, I was loading pack horses at Deer Creek. A thoughtful ranch girl came by. She handed me a small box with a tiny black and gray tiger cat inside. Maggie joined our family. And Tasha's life was never the same again.

Early on, Maggie made it clear that she thought she was better than the dogs. Dogs were to keep their place. If they didn't, they were to be spit at and their noses were to be raked by her sharp claws. Dogs had to stay on the floor. She could curl up on a pillow on the settee, up high where she could look down on the dogs.

Maggie thought the best way to get along with the dogs was to keep them on the defense. Anytime she walked across the cabin floor, she considered it normal feline tactics to jump at a tail or to try to bloody a nose.

I don't know why the dogs put up with her. They could have chewed her up and swallowed her down with one gulp.

Soon Maggie had Skipper fully under control. Whenever he saw the growing kitten coming his way, his eyes got big and showed almost all white. With furtive glances over his shoulder, he moved out of the way. After that, Maggie let Skipper alone. It gave her more time to concentrate on annoying Tasha.

I have no right to say that Tasha hated Maggie. It is probably more proper to say that Tasha developed such an intense dislike for the kitten that it bordered on the neurotic.

I remember one evening well. As was to her liking, Tasha stretched out full length on the floor in front of the stove. With her eyes closed, the dog napped. Maggie came along and stationed herself at the end of Tasha's nose. She did nothing to molest the sleeping dog. Maggie just sat and stared at Tasha's closed eyes.

I suppose Tasha could sense that all was not well. Soon she opened an eye and saw Maggie sitting at the end of her nose. Tasha growled and shifted her head. She closed her eye and again tried to doze.

Now Maggie rolled on her side. Tasha's pointed ears were so close at hand. The kitten reached out a velvety paw and touched one ever so gently. With eyes still closed, the dog flicked the ear as if to get rid of a fly. Maggie waited a full minute before trying it again. With that, the big dog came alive with a start and snapped her white teeth inches away from the head of the kitten.

Unruffled, Maggie rolled to her feet. With her tail pointed straight up, the kitten sauntered to her water dish and started to drink.

Tasha grumbled deep in her throat and looked daggers at the young cat. Moving to a new place on the floor at the head of the settee, the dog stretched out and soon went to sleep.

For want of something better to do, Maggie hopped up on her pillow, high up on the settee. There she licked and washed herself from her head to the tip of her tail.

Now, coming up from the floor, some interesting noises caught Maggie's ear. The kitten crept to the edge of the settee and looked down. Tasha was still stretched out and fast asleep. But the dog was dreaming. She whimpered and panted hard, moving her feet as if she was running in place.

The noises and movements made by the dog seemed to arouse Maggie's primitive instincts. The kitten's eyes brightened with excitement. With her belly pressed flat against the cushions on the settee, she inched forward for a better look. The tip of the young she-cat's tail moved slowly from side to side. Her muscles bunched. She waited no longer. With easy grace, she launched herself into the air. Instinctively her feet clawed for a hold as she landed high on the shoulders of the sleeping dog.

Tasha yelped in surprise. Bounding to her feet, she was instantly awake. With a snarl and a snap, the dog turned on the young cat.

Terrified now, Maggie looked for escape. With one fluid motion, she quit Tasha's back. Landing feet first, she sought and found refuge under a bed.

ø ø ø

That first winter as Maggie grew in size, her relationship

with the dogs improved some, too. Mary had something to do with that. Anytime Mary caught Maggie annoying either of the dogs, she smacked the cat on the behind with the fly swatter. Maggie got the message.

By the time green grass returned to the high country, Mary was often abroad looking for those first newly-bloomed wildflowers. And, more often than not, Maggie followed along. That was when Mary first noticed that Maggie had a very low opinion of coyote sanitary habits. Whenever Maggie came upon coyote scats along the dim trails, she stopped and sniffed disdainfully. Then reaching out with a front paw, the young cat meticulously raked pine needles and other forest duff over the scats until they could no longer be seen. That done, Maggie continued on her way with a self-satisfied look on her feline face. In the months that followed, we observed Maggie conduct this ritual repeatedly whenever she came upon coyote scat.

Although Maggie's deportment had improved, she was still too big for her breeches. She made that clear to Mary and me one evening in June. We were sitting out on the porch sharing thoughts and just taking in the sights and sounds of the place where we live. Keeping us company were the two dogs and Maggie.

From out of the timber west of the cabin, came a lone mule deer doe. She looked our way and took in the scene at a glance. The doe saw nothing that disturbed her sense of security. She grazed selectively across the grassy park and then effortlessly cleared the fence around our camp. Once inside, the deer went directly to the patches of white clover along the spring runoff.

From the porch, Mary and I and the dogs watched the deer with just casual interest. Long ago it had been made clear to our dogs that the elk and deer had as much right to the mountain as they did. But from her place on the porch rail, Maggie indicated that her interest in the doe was something more than casual. Her alert eyes followed every move of the deer. Below the rail, her tail moved slowly in a long arc. Swapping talk with Mary, my eyes left the cat for a moment or so. When they turned that way again, Maggie was gone.

The mule deer fed in the manner grass eaters are known to do. Head down, big ears flicking, short tail jerking, the doe nipped off the tender stems of clover and grass. When her mouth was filled to capacity, the deer lifted her head, and looked around for signs that spoke of danger. That done, she sent the wad of chewed-up clover and grass on its way to her paunch. Again, the head of the doe went down.

From our vantage point, we now saw that a small drama of the high country was about to unfold. Through the tall grass, we made out the black and gray markings of a tiger cat. Her long body stretched out, her belly close to the ground, Maggie stalked the mule deer doe. Each time the deer lowered her head to feed, the young cat quickly and silently stole ahead a few yards or so. Whenever the mule deer lifted her head to look around, the tiger cat became as fixed and silent as a stone.

Once more the mule deer lowered her head. A step at a time she worked to a place where the timothy grew rank and thick. There the doe nipped off green basal leaves of the plant. We knew that from Maggie's viewpoint the stand of timothy would seem like a jungle. And, although she could no longer see the doe, her keen ears picked up the sounds of the animal she stalked. Guided by those sounds, the she-cat knew when to move, when to stop, and when to patiently wait.

Ahead of the cat, the mule deer again lifted her head to look around. She glanced our way and saw nothing to cause her alarm. But now across the small meadow came a gentle

breeze that moved the heads and leaves of the grass. The doe's head became fixed. Her jaws stopped working. Unchewed grass stuck out of her mouth like green whiskers. With nose lifted slightly, the mule deer moved it slowly from side to side, sorting out the smells carried by the moving air.

Alerted now, the doe pivoted on her hind legs and faced the way she had just come. Her front feet beat a tattoo on the sod. Stretching her neck, she peered intently through the grass. One deliberate step at a time, the doe followed her nose on her own back trail.

Then hurtling out of the tall grass came the gray and black form of the young she-cat. Her tail fluffed out, terror in her eyes, Maggie headed our way in ground-covering bounds of six feet or more. Close behind her came the doe. Head carried low, ears pinned back, the mule deer gained on the cat. From the porch, people and dogs had a very good view of the race.

Tearing under the hitch rail in front of the cabin, Maggie held a short lead. A few long bounds and the cat was safe under the cabin.

The mule deer doe pulled up at the hitch rail. She shook her head and stamped her feet. Our two dogs whined and moved about. Mary quietly opened the door, and they hastily scooted inside.

Later as darkness settled on the little meadow near our cabin, I saw the dim form of the mule deer doe. She was nipping off clover as busy as could be.

As for Maggie—we haven't known her to ever stalk a mule deer again.

# Summer Trails

J UST A FAINT GLOW OF sunrise-pink colored the eastern sky
when I rode out of camp. And I felt enough nip in the
morning air to make me glad for my wool jacket, gloves
and chinks. Bridger, with head up and ears alert, was moving
out in his comfortable, ground-eating stride. Close at
Bridger's heels, Skipper trotted along on his short legs. The
dog never seemed to have any trouble keeping up. I don't
know how he did it.

Later, when the sun had climbed a notch or two, I topped
out on a grassy divide. I got off and snugged up the cinch on
my saddle and looked around. Spread out on the slope below
me was the cut I had dropped there the evening before—
forty-five cows with calves at side and two range bulls.

All areas of this mountain are not ready to be grazed
when the cattle first come to the high country. The grass in the
higher elevations is slower to start. It takes additional days of
sunlight to bring the grass up to grazing height. Snowdrifts
are slow to melt on the high divides. Often they present a bar-
rier to any cattle you might want to trail that way. But the
summer sun is a persistent thing. Each day that a cloudless
sky will allow it, it bears down on those reluctant snowdrifts.
Finally they give up. Then snow water trickles down the slope
to irrigate the range plants below them.

A few days earlier, with two pack horses loaded with salt

and another carrying chain saw, gas and oil and tools, I made a trip into what we call the Dead Horse Country. I cleared blown-down trees off the trail and put out salt in three places where the cattle had been salted before. I scouted around and saw the grass was ready for cattle.

Now with my cut close at hand and the air still cool enough for a good cattle drive, I was ready to start for Dead Horse. Skipper whined at Bridger's heels and looked along the slope. Below us, cows lifted their heads. First they looked up the slope at horse, man and dog. Then with their big ears forward, the cows looked left and right for calves. Some cows bawled. Calves raised their heads, then looked for their mothers. I gave out with a whoop and a holler. Cows called to their calves and moved down the slope. Skipper had already contributed to the project of the day by just being there. Nothing gets a cow to thinking of her calf quicker than the sight of a dog.

With Skipper's help, I rode the edges and threw the bunch together. Loping ahead, I pointed the lead more to the west. A smart old cow led the bunch toward a hole in the pine forest that was the start of the Dead Horse Trail. A few cows and calves talked back and forth, and the two bulls hustled to keep up with the herd. Inside the forest, most of the cattle hit the trail and strung out like they wanted to go. Some of the cattle hung back in a crisscross tangle of down timber. Skipper got around them, and they changed their minds.

It is six miles or so from the start of the trail to where I would drop the herd later. We would skirt a half-dozen swamp meadows on the drive. Other than that, the trail would be timber-lined all the way.

At the drag, some of the cattle bunched up more than they should. I hung back and let them string out. Usually a rider can tell in about fifteen minutes how the cattle are going to trail that day. I liked the way the herd ahead of me acted. They were strung out in a long line, one or two cows wide. I didn't hear much cow-calf talk because just about every one of the cows had her calf moving right at her side. And the way they were going, it didn't make much sense for me to make a lot of noise behind them. Oh, once in a while, I let out a whoop, just to let them know I hadn't turned around and gone back home. A long time ago, a good old cowman told me, "Mark, you just let them take their own time, and you'll make the best time." That's the way I try to do it. However, I expect the cows to make an effort to get along with me, too.

When you've got a herd strung out in a long, thin line on a timber-lined trail, it's hard to be pointing them and pushing them at the same time. A rider has to take a few calculated risks. If a bunch of cows knows where it is going, it helps a lot. They'll usually stay on the trail, that is, unless some rider gets in a hurry and starts to crowd them too hard from behind.

I had only one problem to cause me concern that day. A cow up ahead was wandering around, on and off the trail, as if she couldn't see very well.

I suppose in some circles, nice people would say the cow was "in season." Other people, not as nice, would say she was "in heat." A recent graduate of a school of veterinary medicine would refer to the cow as being "in estrus." The time-worn cowman would simply say, "The old rip is bullin'." If it was early in the breeding season, he might smile. On the first of September, he would shake his head and grunt, "Late calves. Who needs them?"

Whatever her condition might be called, a cow like this is a nuisance on the trail. Among other things, she will turn around and block the trail so other cattle can't get by. The big bull following her does his share of blocking, too. A cow like that doesn't care where her calf is. She has other things on her mind. And her calf usually doesn't know where mama is. So he has thoughts of hitting the back trail to where he nursed last. It helps if a cowboy can just get the calf up where he can sniff his mother's flank once. Then he is more likely to stay with the herd.

We had four divides to climb up and over before we got to Dead Horse. And those divides had a going-down side, too. On the going-down side, I almost always got off and led my horse.

A horse carries about two-thirds of his weight on his front end. It's the front feet and legs of a horse that take the most punishment. And that is where they usually go lame. Most often, in rough country, the injury occurs from the frequent jarring of downhill travel. Unfortunately much of the time, the injury can't be repaired. It means that an otherwise useful horse is lost from the working string of a ranch. Many times heartache is involved, too, at the breakup of a man-horse relationship.

Mary and I have some good horses. We try to stretch their useful lives. That is why we get off and walked down-hill more often than we used to. And the longer and rougher the downhill trail is, the more it makes us aware of the punishment a horse's front end takes. We are sure we help our horses. Sometimes, Mary and I wonder how long it will be before we go lame ourselves.

When the cattle and I came off the first divide down into a draw, we found a small, clear creek running over gravel. The cattle took on some water, not much, because they'd had many opportunities to drink since we started the drive. In general, this high country range is well-watered by live springs and running streams. Most of the cattle hit the trail again and went on without urging. A few are always slow to leave the creek bottoms. Skipper got around those hanging back in the timber. Soon the herd was strung out on the uphill side of the next divide.

Bridger sipped on the cold, clear water, then reached out for the tops of the tall grass. I mounted and got behind the herd. Those range cows, wise to the ways of up-and-down country, knew when to stop and rest. I let them do so. A man doesn't gain much by trying to push too hard on a cow or horse climbing a hill.

The drive was going good. Once in a while, I had to go after the bulling cow and her followers and put them back on the trail. Whenever we skirted those swamp meadows, a few cows always quit the trail to give a try to the rank, water-tolerant grass. Some of those swamps were so boggy it wasn't wise to ride a horse in there. That's when Skipper went to work and put the cows back with the moving herd. The air was still cool. Cows and calves knew where each other were. And usually, that makes for a quiet, steady-moving herd. So it went. Up and over a divide. Down the other side. Splash through a creek.

I was glad to cross that last divide and start the long, gradual descent to Dead Horse Creek. I bet the cattle were, too. There was a steep, little pitch just before we dropped down on the creek bottom. Most of the cows and calves trotted down that hill. The calves played and jumped around. And some of the cows acted silly, like calves, too. In a matter of minutes, the herd was spread out grazing on meadows that hadn't felt a bovine hoof since the fall before.

I watched the herd for awhile. Cows and calves seemed to be mothered-up. Even the calf belonging to the bulling cow got his mother to stand still long enough for him to nurse. I noticed that the two bulls were grazing not far apart.

I thought the cattle looked good. The cows were milking enough and still packing good flesh. Except for a few that were born late, the calves had a growthy look. A lot of the calves I was looking at would weigh over five hundred pounds at weaning time. They probably weighed about seventy-five pounds at birth, and most of them had been gaining over two pounds each day ever since. To get calves to perform like that takes the right kind of genetics, plus the right kind of feed for cow and calf. And, most importantly, that feed can't cost too much or you can't pay off at the bank—even with heavy calves.

Skipper went off to check on rockchucks he hadn't seen since the year before. Robins hopped along just about the way they do any other place. Munching on a sandwich, I gazed out across the glassy surface of a small pond, formed at a bend in the creek. I've only seen wild ducks on that sub-alpine water a couple of times. I miss them.

That 3:30 A.M. get-up time was catching up with me. The midday sun made me sleepy, so I stretched out under a Douglas fir. Pulling my hat down over my eyes, I tried to doze. But that wasn't to be. Mosquitos landed in a thirsty swarm. I didn't mind the blood they took. It was the noise they made that kept me awake. I put my hands behind my head and watched Bridger nip grass just below me. The sun struck his chocolate-sorrel hide just right to make it shine.

I thought back to the days when Bridger joined my string as a three-year-old. That was when Alkali Rob was riding the colts for the ranch. Rob had him going nicely, then one day he tied him in my stall in the horse barn at Deer Creek. I kept Bridger in that first winter and gave him enough oats to match the work he was doing. The sorrel colt continued to grow.

One winter day I was riding Bridger when Gabby, a rider at Deer Creek, and I were moving a small bunch of cows to Beetle Creek. We were almost there when a sudden snow squall hit hard. In a few minutes, all landmarks were lost to view, but I knew the gate to the pasture was up ahead, someplace close.

I loped through a wall of goose-down snowflakes to open the gate so the cows could go through. Peering past Bridger's ears I saw a snowdrift, but I saw it too late. It was made of old, packed, crusted snow, and it gripped Bridger's front legs like a trap. The colt fell on his side, and I went with him.

My left leg was under the horse. My right foot was free of the stirrup. Bridger tried to get up. I was concerned that my left foot might be hung up in the stirrup. I tried to hold Bridger's head down, so he couldn't get to his feet. I had lost my reins in the fall, and I couldn't reach the bridle to get a good hand hold.

Bridger thrashed around then lunged to his feet. My left foot was free of the stirrup, but I found myself dangling from the horse's left side. The saddle horn was hooked on some part of my chaps. I knew if I was caught by the light leather string that goes across the front of the chaps, it would have broken already and I would have fallen free. But I was held fast. My toes couldn't quite touch the ground. I couldn't pull myself aboard, and I couldn't free myself and drop to the ground.

Through all this, Bridger, the coming four-year-old, stood firm. I hated to think what would happen if the colt spooked and then stampeded across the country with me hanging on his side. The saddle could slip and that would make it worse.

By now, the cows had caught up with us and were milling around the horse because the gate wasn't open to let them through. In a minute Gabby rode out of the thick, falling

snow. He sized up the situation at a glance. Gabby swung off his horse and came my way, moving carefully, deliberately. Gabby got his shoulder under my rear end and lifted. I wiggled and pulled as much as I could. When I got on top, I found myself on the horse's neck, not in the saddle. I could see the saddle horn had gone down along my thigh into the top of one shotgun chap. But at least now, I could use two hands. With Gabby's help, I got free of the saddle horn and let myself slide to the ground.

I thanked Gabby for getting me out of the jackpot. Stepping forward, I picked up my reins. Then putting my arms around Bridger's neck, I thanked him, too.

Now years later, I walked down to the tall, sorrel horse, and I picked up my reins. Reaching up, I put my arms around Bridger's neck and thanked him again. Climbing aboard, I headed for home.

# Little Stories About Animals

I TRAILED A BUNCH of cattle to Frying Pan Creek—not a big bunch, thirty pairs and a bull. They spread out on the slope below me, some working the salt lick, a few still taking on a fill of fresh grass. Most had been to the creek for water and were now lying down in the shade of a stand of quaking aspen.

Higher up the slope, I shaded up myself under the thick branches of a blue spruce. Stretched out full length, I wiggled around a bit to get settled in the cushiony carpet of forest duff. Then letting my head come to rest against the trunk of the tree, I was ready to eat lunch and see what I could see.

Happy Jack, my horse of the day, grazed close to the stand of aspens. Looking beyond the horse, I saw a calf come out of the shade. He wasn't one of the biggest calves, but the way he moved and carried his head, I figured he might be one of the cockiest. Another calf came by. Cocky shook his head and bounced around, encouraging the other calf to play. But that calf had no time for play. He had spied his mother, and he trotted to her side for a lunch of warm milk.

Cocky looked around, his ears alert, searching for any adventure that might come his way. The calf saw Happy Jack grazing close by. Cocky bounded toward the horse and came to a stiff-legged stop inches away from the grazing horse's nose. Happy Jack never lifted his head.

Victoria 1990

Cocky bounced up and down and to the left and right. The horse continued to graze. The calf moved closer and put his head against that of the horse. Cocky pushed his head hard against the horse's head. The calf's neck bowed; his hind feet scratched at the ground. The calf might as well have been pushing against the trunk of a tree. Happy Jack shook his head as if to get rid of a fly. Cocky backed off, then moved to the hind end of the horse.

The sorrel horse turned his head to follow the course of the calf. Satisfied, he continued to nip off grass.

Cocky backed up a step or two, then charged. All business, he butted the hind legs of the horse. Happy Jack never lifted a hoof. Cocky found himself with his head between the hocks of the horse. Moving his head up and down, he rubbed each side of his neck. That done, he saw the tail of the horse hanging conveniently near. Rotating his head, he washed his face all over. Then looking around, he left the horse. Still cocky and on the prowl for mischief, he trotted toward some cows and calves.

ø ø ø

Through the years, other calves have given me cause to chuckle and a story to relate to Mary when I got back to the house at night.

One day I was moving a bunch of cows and calves. Riding down a draw, I gave a whoop and a holler once in a while, and the cattle gathered themselves and moved along. All I had to do was follow. But from long habit, I turned in my saddle and glanced back at the country we had just left. Sure enough, at the edge of a brush patch, I saw the red and white markings of a Hereford calf. Not all the calves had moved with the herd.

I trotted back to bring him along. The calf never lifted his head as I rode up. He was too busy at a task he had taken on for himself. Right under his nose lay a recently born mule deer fawn. With his mother off looking for feed, the fawn was hugging the ground "playing dead." Not even an eyelash moved.

The calf never slowed down in his task. He was busy licking the fawn with his coarse tongue. I don't know how long he had been there showing his affection, but I could see the fawn was wet from head to tail. Just behind the fawn's left foreleg, I could see his thin, spotted hide rising and falling rapidly in rhythm to his pulsing heart. No doubt the young deer was frightened, but instinct told him, that at his tender age, his best protection was to "play dead."

The mother of the calf trotted up about the time I gave a spook to her youngster. She bawled once and he joined her, and the pair hustled to catch up with the herd.

ø ø ø

I've got some other little stories cached away in the back of my head. If you've got time to listen, I'll dig out a few.

Some years back, Mary and I rode up to the cow camp. It was late afternoon in the middle of May. From the look of the trail, I would say we were the first people up since the fall before.

Off to the north and below us was a nice little aspen pocket with good grass and water. I spoke to Mary. "You know, of all the times I've been up and down this trail, I've never seen an elk in that pocket."

Mary reined in her horse. She lifted our big binoculars from her saddlebag and glassed the country. "How about settling for a bear?" she asked.

I took the binoculars and looked myself. "How about settling for two bears?" I said. Sure enough, a black cub had just come out from a thicket to join his equally black mother.

We looked some more, but all we could see was the sow and her cub. So we rode on up the trail.

The next evening with the light still holding good, we

rode back down. "I wonder if we'll see our friends?" Mary asked, her voice low. She pulled up her horse and used the binoculars as she had the day before.

Mary kept the binoculars longer than I thought was her share. When she did hand them over, she was smiling broadly. "Take a look," she said.

Mary was right. The black sow had been joined by another mature black bear and a cinnamon cub. Both big bears were busy turning over rocks, looking for grubs or ants or anything else that looked good to eat. To this day, I don't know if both cubs belonged to the sow we had seen the day before or if one belonged to the second mature bear. I only know they were there.

With the help of the binoculars, I glanced farther up the slope. I sucked in my breath and smiled. Not far above the four bears were seven grazing elk. They looked like young females, too young to have calves. I thought, well, at least I've finally seen elk in that pocket.

Close to my ear, Mary spoke. "Keep looking, Mark."

I looked some more and saw what I should have seen when I spotted the elk. Close to the elk were two coyotes. The 9-X binoculars brought them my way. The coyotes were busy pouncing on mice that the grazing elk were driving their way. It was as if the elk were serving them supper.

Mary took the binoculars and enjoyed the peaceful scene a while longer. Then leaving the bears, and the elk, and the coyotes to share the mountain, we rode on down the trail.

⊘ ⊘ ⊘

Another time, close to twenty years ago, I hustled off the face of the mountain, trying to get home before dark. There were no trails in the area. I traveled on snowshoes over a couple feet of settled snow. The temperature was probably about zero.

Down the steep slope not far off my course, I knew of a shallow cave well hidden in the timber. I had often thought that sometime the place might have to furnish me shelter. I had only been there once, so I thought it might be well to get acquainted again.

About that time, it started to snow, and a brisk wind drove small flakes across the face of the mountain. I didn't feel I had reason to need the shelter of the cave that evening, but I still felt it would be wise to check it out.

Traveling on a switchback route, I lost elevation rapidly. I picked up a couple of landmarks I remembered and came out on a point from where I could look down on the shallow cave. It resembled an open cattle shed. A rimrock hanging far out formed the roof. I guessed the cave to be about forty feet long and nine or ten feet deep. The floor of the shelter was almost free of snow.

I chuckled to myself as I took in the scene. If I planned to use the shelter that night, I would have to share it with other occupants trying to get out of the storm. At one end of the cave stood a mule deer doe and her fawn of last spring. At the other end, a full grown coyote sat on his haunches. The two deer and the coyote looked out at the storm and seemed more interested in the weather than in each other.

I thought three might be company, but four would be a crowd. I turned and hustled down the slope.

ø ø ø

It is a horse's nature to take notice of the new, strange things he comes in contact with. And, it is a trait of certain horses to be more suspicious than most. Some horses almost seem to enjoy looking for unusual things to fret about. For instance, there was the black horse Buckshot.

I was saddling up pack horses at the cow camp corral early one summer morning. I saddled Buckshot first so he could soak for awhile and tied him to the corral fence. As I worked with the other horses, I noticed that Buckshot kept looking out across the horse pasture toward the east gate. The black horse lifted his head. He snorted through his nose and danced at the end of his tie rope. I thought Mary might be coming over to give me a message. Maybe Buckshot didn't recognize Mary for who she was. No one came.

I went on with my work. Buckshot kept fussing. Soon I saw a coyote trotting along the east side of the pasture. The coyote stopped and looked our way, then moved on down the creek and out of sight. Well, that ought to take care of Buckshot's problem, I mused.

I finished saddling Sleepy and went to get another horse. Buckshot continued to fuss, only worse. I glanced over toward the east. A mule deer buck drifted along the creek. He looked our way and hesitated, then hurried on in the wake of the coyote. Well, that's probably it, I supposed. Maybe Buckshot's sight was failing and he thought the buck was a dinosaur or something.

But the problem was still not solved. Buckshot continued to look east. He snorted worse than ever and started to sweat, and he never left four feet on the ground at the same time. By then, I was getting curious myself and just a bit irked. From the corral, I peered intently out across the pasture. I saw nothing that should spook a horse. But, for sure, Buckshot thought something was there, maybe down in the grass where I couldn't see it.

I stopped my work with the other horses and started to walk slowly across the pasture, looking for whatever was causing the trouble. About forty yards out from the corral, I halted myself and looked carefully ahead. Not far from the end of my nose something flashed in the sunlight and disappeared. Waiting, I pulled the brim of my hat down lower and peered intently ahead. A light breeze brushed my cheek. The thing flashed again and disappeared. I was stumped. Not moving a step, I stretched my neck out like a suspicious horse. Straining my eyes, I searched for the thing. All at once, I laughed.

At eyeball height, an industrious spider had stretched his web between two trees. Every time the elastic filament swayed in the gentle breeze, it picked up sunlight and sent silver-white flashes Buckshot's way.

I broke the web with my hand and walked back to the corral. Buckshot looked out across the pasture with a sort of puzzled expression on his face. Soon the horse stood quietly.

 Downslope Trails

T HERE COMES A TIME when the signs of early fall make
their subtle showing on the high country. Except for
those places along the seep springs and in the marshes,
the range grass turns a somber brown. But there is nothing
somber about the bluebells, the purple asters and the golden-
rod still holding sway on the mountain. A bit of red is added
by the frost-touched leaves of wild strawberry and raspberry.
Then depending on elevation, the leaves of the quaking
aspen make a splash of bright yellow against the green of
coniferous forest.

Black and white magpies fly up from the low country for
a short stay. Among other places, those brazen, squawking
birds visit our camp. They like to clean up around the dog
dishes outside. Tasha doesn't mind if the gray jays do that, but
she chases the magpies away. Maybe she figures the gray jays
belong to our family.

One day moves into another. In the morning, along the
edge of a muddy creek crossing, I find thin ice bridging holes
punched by the hoofs of cattle. Then one day, I realize the
robins and juncos have quit the mountaintop. A week later the
mountain bluebirds gather in restless flocks. Then they, too,
take off in flight toward a warmer climate.

Saddling up in the morning, I notice the horses have
started to grow winter hair. That evening riding toward home,

I hear the clear, bugle-like call a bull elk sends out to announce the start of the rut. Those stirring sounds ricocheting off the canyon walls tell us, like nothing else, that early fall has, indeed, moved in on the high country.

Fall days are busy days for Mary and me. We like to have all our logs skidded in by the first of September. Some years we haven't met that target date. It is a happy day for me when I come down the hill with the last of over a hundred logs. That number of logs will take care of our firewood and minor construction needs for a year. And when I pull the harness off our skid horse for the last time and turn him out with the bunch, I bet it is a happy day for him, too.

By the middle of September, Mary has purchased all but a few of the items we will need for a six or seven month snowed-in winter. Much of it has already been packed up the mountain by Mary or me. Some of it is stored in our tack room at Deer Creek. That stuff is properly boxed and weighed, ready to load on a pack horse. That makes it handy for me whenever I get a chance to go down.

Mary makes the most of the remaining fair weather we have on the mountain. With a bucket in hand, she hustles  from one wild raspberry patch to another. She wants to harvest as many of those berries as she can before a hard frost causes them to fall to the ground. Mary doesn't have to compete with just the frost. The cows, elk, deer, squirrels, birds, and even the coyotes try to beat Mary to those zesty wild raspberries. The proof that she gathers her share is seen by the jars of jelly on the shelves in our back storeroom.

Most of my own time is spent riding over a sizeable

piece of high country range. I ask myself questions like these: Is there enough salt out to take care of the needs of the cattle until the end of the season? How is the grass holding up on the different areas of the range? Should some bunch be moved to another place where the feed is better?

It is almost impossible to get an accurate tally of the cattle as you ride the range. But a rider can come close enough to get an idea where the stock is working. I like to know where the bulls are, as it tells me something about the rest of the cattle, too.

In the fall, it is common to find cattle wearing a brand that doesn't belong on the range I'm riding. They have drifted off allotments many miles away. I try to get word to the owners of those strays. Then they won't spend long days looking for a bull or a few cows that quit their own summer range long ago. Strays go off the mountain with whatever herd they join up with. The owner then cuts them out on the county road or picks them up in a truck at some rancher's corral.

The season moves along. We wake up some morning to find a few inches of snow on the ground. I swap my Stetson for my Scotch cap, and I keep my jacket on all day.

Our horses are ready for their last shoeing of the season. Even though the ground is mostly snow-free, we have them shod with winter calks, and a plastic snow pad is put under the shoe. We know what to expect in the way of weather, but we don't know when to expect it.

The range boss sets a date for the association cattle to be gathered and moved off the mountain. As that time gets close, I ride the back country and throw in whatever cattle I can find. A few more days go by. As best I can, I sort the cattle according to brand. A couple of ranchers find it convenient to take their cattle home by way of Powderhorn Canyon. I push those herds that way. The other outfits join up and move off by going down the Gunshot Trail.

Down in the low country, the cattle are sorted along county roads. Finally, each rancher trails the cattle wearing his brand back home. A more accurate count is made of the cattle that came off the mountain. In a couple of days, the range boss gets word to me as to how many head each outfit is short. Some ranchers may not be short any cattle. Other outfits may be short a single calf or a bull or as many as a half-dozen cow-calf pairs.

I scratch my head and try to think where the ornery critters might be. They might have drifted off their own range and already have gone off the mountain with some other herd. But that outfit would have gotten word to the owners by now. So they must still be up here on the summer range.

This is a big, rough country with plenty of remote places cattle might find to their liking. With the weather still holding mild, cattle would have no reason to think of going home. Those bovine hideouts could be in one bunch. Or they might be scattered in three or four places, with only a couple of head to each place. Wherever they are, it is my job to find them and get them home where they belong. Sometimes there is no real urgency. But if a rancher has contracted his calves to be sold and delivered on a certain date, he wants those calves where he can put them across a scale. And he can't do that if they are still on top of the mountain.

ø ø ø

One year there was a two-year-old Hereford bull on this range that I liked very much. About a month before the cattle were to be moved off the mountain, the bull turned up missing. At first I wasn't too concerned about not seeing him. I thought the next time I rode I would surely see him, following along behind the herd he was supposed to be with. That wasn't to be. I kept my eyes peeled for the son-of-a-gun, but when the cattle went off the mountain, the bull wasn't with them. By that time, I had begun to wonder if he was lying dead under a spruce tree.

It turned out the outfit that owned the bull was short two cow-calf pairs, in addition to the bull. That gave me something to go on.

Every morning, mounted on a fresh horse, I would start out to scour the country. I rode the most likely places until there weren't any more likely places left.

Then one morning under leaden skies, I left Shonto Park and started out on the Dead Horse Trail. Skipper trotted close behind. Only a few inches of snow covered the frozen ground. Thin sheets of ice lay along the edges of the small creeks that Kyska, the big sorrel, splashed through. Skipper rock-hopped. It was a cold, sunless trip to Dead Horse Creek. The only time I warmed up was when I led my horse downhill.

When I got there, I rode up the creek about three miles, looking for cattle sign around the salt licks and on the bog meadows along the creek. I concluded there hadn't been a bovine beast in that country since the bunch I had picked up ten days before.

Riding back down the creek, I racked my brain trying to figure out where I should look next for the bull and the cows with him, if there really were cattle with him. At the foot of the trail leading back to Shonto Park, I pulled up my horse. Staring down at the top of my saddle horn, I did some hard thinking. Then, my decision made, I reined Kyska around and rode down the creek. I would ride toward home through the heart of the Tanglefoot Country.

A quarter mile later, I left the creek and pointed my horse toward the north. I followed a dim trail through a chain of small parks, then started to climb a fairly open hogback ridge. From there I could look down on either side into draws that reached up toward the higher country and then petered out.

Head down, ironshod feet scratching, Kyska carried me higher. Finally we topped out on a rocky viewpoint. I gazed across a large, dark green, forested country. The land was cut by sharp ridges and deep draws, falling away toward the distant West Fork of the Powderhorn. From where I was looking, I couldn't see signs of enough grass to carry a saddle horse overnight. But I knew down each of those draws an unnamed creek flowed through dank, grassy swamps and alongside small parks where grass grew up between granite boulders.

My experience with the Tanglefoot Country had been that in spite of the grass that grew there, cattle shunned the place. The few cattle that drifted that way never lingered long. I think they must consider it a spooky place. But still, wherever grass grew, there was always a chance there might be cattle. I would take a look.

I didn't have time to ride up and down each of those draws. It would take a few days to get that done. Keeping to a rough northerly course, I crossed each of those draws as I slid off the ridge behind me. Bottoming out along a small creek, I scouted for cow tracks in the light cover of snow.

So it went. Climb up and over a ridge. Pick and slide my way down the other side. A blue grouse flew up under Kyska's feet and landed on the lower limb of a dead pine. From the middle of a swamp, a lone cow moose shook her head at Skipper and watched us go by. She probably had a calf hidden out not far away.

Searching the ground for cattle sign, I worked my way down another draw. At a place where the draw widened to form a thirty acre meadow, I found tracks. At first I thought some elk had passed that way. Soon I saw sign that told me it was cattle that had been on that meadow the day before.

My spirits picked up. I felt like baying the way a hound

dog bays. I put Kyska into a shuffle and rode the length of the meadow until it ended in a grove of aspen. I could see a few cattle had bedded down there the night before. I picked up a fresh trail leading through the timber close to the creek. In about five minutes, the country opened up again. On a small meadow, tall, brown grass stood above snow cover. Lying down near a bend in the creek, a little bunch of cattle bent their ears my way. I pulled up my horse. Talking quietly, I let them look me over good. Then I rode closer.

The bull I had been hunting for over a month gazed my way through placid, half-closed eyes. His muzzle lifted slightly, and he chewed his cud as though he didn't have a care in the world. Nearby lay two cow-calf pairs from the same herd and a black yearling heifer with a tag in her ear. The yearling got to her feet. I recognized her brand as that belonging to an outfit that summered cattle far from here. How they all got together, and where they had been for the past month or so, I didn't know.

I whistled once and waved an arm. The rest of the cattle got to their feet and they stretched out of shape. Then I started them down the creek. Sooner or later, we would drop down on the West Fork of the Powderhorn. An old cow took the lead. She moved out like she wanted to go home now, and the rest of the bunch strung out behind her. Skipper trotted along at the drag.

It started to snow. Big, sticky flakes landed on my nose. Soon it built up on the pommel of my saddle. I brushed it off before it slid under the seat of my pants. I tightened the drawstring on my parka hood and kept my eyes on the bobbing heads of those home-bent cattle.

The cow in the lead seemed to know where she was going, but she hadn't spent much time surveying the road. The fall of the land became more steep, and the creek made the noise of a tumbling, plunging stream. The old cow led us through places where spindly lodgepole pine grew thick as hair on a dog's back. At times, the side of the draw closed in. Marshes of black, sucking mud spread from creek bank to sheer cliff. I had to get off and lead my horse up and around high rocky points where the trail was more fit for a mountain goat than a horse or a cow. But where the old cow led, the rest of us followed.

An hour and a half passed by. Then out of the curtain of snow and below us, I heard the sound of a bigger and louder stream. In a few minutes, we slid down a steep, little pitch. Close by, I saw the rushing, white water of West Fork tumbling over black boulders.

The lead cow never slowed down. On a shelf above the creek, she followed a hoof-worn trail that went the way of the turbulent water.

The snow came down heavier. I didn't mind. I was headed toward home and had my cattle strung out ahead of me.

ø ø ø

Some years the signs of fall don't come in a subtle way. They come suddenly, with all the violence that a Rocky Mountain snowstorm can lash out with.

For instance, there was that early storm a couple years ago. In early September, we had summer-like weather. I scheduled my work of packing in supplies or trailing cattle as if it were July. A man had to get an early start to beat the heat of the mid-day sun.

The cattle on all parts of the range had a good spread. In the back country, cows and calves and bulls shaded up by mid-morning and gave no thoughts to going home to low country pastures.

On September 11, storm clouds started to build up around the tall peaks. But the weather was still warm. I rode the whole day without a jacket, and at times, wished I had worn a straw hat instead of a Stetson.

During the night things changed. The wind started to blow, and I heard snow beating against the windowpanes. In the morning, there were a few inches of snow on the ground. It snowed all day, but it never built up to more than three or four inches. The ground was warm, so the snow melted almost as fast as it landed. Whatever cattle I saw that day were scattered nicely and seemed content to push their muzzles down through four inches of wet snow to get to cured grass.

That night the snow still fell, and the temperature dropped. In the morning, we measured eight inches of snow on the ground, with more coming down every minute. I rode to the drift-fence gate on Shonto Creek at the upper end of Shonto Park. I saw cattle there I hadn't seen the day before. The storm had brought them out of the back country. I recognized a bull and several cows I had last seen on Dead Horse Creek. They had come out on a six-mile trail during the night with thoughts of going home. I made a rough count of all the cattle I could see. Some had come from Pecos Park, and a small bunch had come over the divide from Agate Creek Valley. Still my count told me not all the cattle at that end of the range were thinking of going home.

I swung my horse around and started up the long slope toward the cow camp to catch a fresh horse. The snow was wet and heavy. I was glad we had snow pads under the shoes on all our horses. Those pads kept the snow from balling up under the horse's hoof; thus, the winter calks could get down and make contact where they could do some good.

Going over a rise, I pulled up my horse to let him take a blow. Waiting, I looked toward the west and Agate Creek Divide. I squinted my eyes and peered hard through the falling snow. I saw what I hoped I wouldn't see. Coming over the divide was a long, thin line of home-bent cattle, every bobbing head pointed toward the drift-fence gate.

By now, over a foot of snow had accumulated on the ground, and it was still coming down. I changed horses at the cow camp and rode other parts of the range. Helped by the fall of the terrain, some bunches of cattle could get to lower country where the snow was less of a problem.

When I went to bed that night it was still snowing. In the morning, two feet of snow was on the ground, with large, flat snowflakes falling fast. A light wind had come up during the night, and the temperature had dropped to 15 degrees.

Before breakfast, I went out to find Happy Jack, the horse I would ride that day. I found the sorrel gelding, shaking and shivering, in the lee of an Engelmann spruce. The horse was plastered with snow. Icicles hung down from his belly and from the hair along his jaw and muzzle.

We have no barn at this camp. I tied Happy Jack to the hitch rail near our saddle rack and used the curry comb sparingly that morning. The snow and ice seemed to be glued to the horse.

Happy Jack is usually a gentle horse. But that morning he humped up and laid his ears back when he felt the weight of the saddle. After saddling, I covered the horse from his ears to his tail with a heavy tarp. I secured it with a light rope around his middle. I gave Jack a generous ration of grain cake and some hay cubes. Then I went in to eat my own breakfast.

Mary and I listened to the weather report on the radio. They didn't promise any letup in the storm. I also contacted the range boss on our communication radio and conferred with him about what was going on up here.

After breakfast, I went out and removed the tarp I had put over Happy Jack. When I snugged up my saddle cinch, he laid back his ears and turned his head my way as though he had thoughts of taking a bite out of my arm. I turned him around a few times, then swung aboard. I could feel the hump in his back right up through the seat of my pants. The sorrel wouldn't move out of his tracks. I talked him out of bucking. He loosened up, and we rode off into the storm.

Horse travel was slow that morning. Heavy as the snow was, the wind was still blowing it some. Where drifts had built up, Happy Jack had to lunge to get through. Visibility was poor. At times, I got off and led my horse. I had no wish to ride, unsuspecting, into a snow-covered gully. I was glad I had left Skipper home that day.

Whenever one of these early storms hits the high country, the cowmen hope the storm will soon quit, that the sun will come out and melt the snow. Then their cattle can get a couple weeks more of mountaintop grass.

It didn't look as though this storm was going to do that. The cattle I was most concerned about were those above the Shonto Creek drift fence. They would stand there and shrink. I would turn the Shonto Creek cattle loose that day.

Later when I rode up to the drift-fence gate, every bovine head was turned my way. Many more cattle had come out of the back country. Each critter was plastered with snow and had a hump in its back. I got off and opened the gate.

A couple of range-wise cows turned toward their calves and lowed softly. When they moved toward the gate, the calves traveled at their sides. Soon a steady stream of cows, calves, and bulls filed through the gate. They needed no urging; they knew the way home. I'd already set the gates and broken out a trail through the deep snow. They had a clear shot to the foot of the mountain.

With that herd on its way, I pointed Happy Jack toward Bearbait Creek. He wasn't eager to go. The horse was ready to head for home. Out in the open, the wind came our way.

Snow rode that wind, smashing against my nose and cheeks. Happy Jack turned his head and ducked his chin until it almost touched his chest. Still the horse forged ahead, through snow two to three feet deep.

An hour later, I picked up tracks of a herd of cattle. The trail was not over five minutes old. The tracks told the story that the herd had traveled to the drift-fence gate at the end of Cougar Mountain. Finding it closed, they had turned back and were now heading up for the shelter of Bearbait Draw. I could do better than that for those drifting cows.

I pushed my horse as hard as I dared. Soon, I caught up with the herd and got around them. I pointed my horse at the leaders. Waving the coil of my lariat in the air and hollering until my voice was about to crack, I got those snow-plastered cattle stopped and turned. Once turned, they strung out on their own back trail.

With a broken-out trail to travel on, the cows moved right along. Following in their wake, Happy Jack had the easiest going he'd had all day.

I put the herd through the gate. Shortly, the cattle would drop down into a draw where aspen groves offered shelter and where tall timothy grass grew along a free-flowing creek. In the morning, they could work their way lower into Powderhorn Canyon and further on toward home.

The next day, the snow stopped falling. The sun came out and bore down on the moisture-heavy snow on the ground. In the low country, ranchers had picked up the cattle I had started off the mountain. It took me a few days to gather up the stragglers who had found shelter wherever they could. I turned them down the trail. Then word came back up the mountain that all the ranchers had their cattle back home.

That's the way it was a couple of years ago when a Rocky Mountain snowstorm struck early in the fall.

 Snow Moon

FALL DAYS ARE UNPREDICTABLE. The snow comes down and the temperature drops. Then the sun comes out to settle the snow. The temperature goes up, and the open slopes facing south bare off. But whatever the weather may be, the work of fall goes on.

For several years, in the fall I received well over a hundred yearling heifers to go on a private mountain pasture owned by the ranch. They came from a nine-thousand-foot range to the west, a two-day trail drive from here. At the end of the first day, the riders from the ranch got the yearlings bedded down along a creek and crawled into bedrolls themselves. The next morning they hit the trail and came this way.

One fall I saddled up by Coleman lantern and headed west to lend a hand. No moon lit the way, but Nugget knew every twist and turn in the trail, and Skipper trotted close behind. All I had to do was to remember to duck for low limbs. Once in awhile, Nugget snorted at something back in the shadows and danced sideways a step or two. But most of the time, the tall, brown horse looked straight ahead and made far-apart tracks in the crunchy snow.

The sun was about halfway over to noon when we picked our way along Digger Creek. Odd name, I thought. I wondered who had named the creek long ago and how they arrived at that name. About that time, I thought I heard the faint sound of a bell. I pulled up my horse and listened again. Sure enough, echoing down from the granite crags above the trail came the crystal clear sounds of Swiss mountain music. Nugget nickered and looked around.

I rode around a bend and peered ahead. In the distance, I could see the herd of yearling heifers just starting to string through a small, rocky saddle. They were a silent herd. No cow-calf talk in that bunch. The heifers just followed along with faith in the music man in the lead.

In this case, the music man's name is Snowball. Snowball is a big, black steer. He has a good job. Snowball spends the summer on the mountain surrounded by pretty bovine lassies. All he has to do is carry that Swiss bell from a strap around his neck and lead those heifers wherever he is told.

Henry was the one who first thought of using a bell steer to lead those yearlings on that two-day drive from the Tin Cup Range. That was after an earlier trip when Henry had said, "The only time they were on the trail was when they crossed it. They need a leader."

That winter Henry halter-broke and gentled down the black steer. That Holstein-Angus cross would never see a stock show, but he got as much petting and pampering as if he was going to the National Western in January. It wasn't long before Henry had Snowball leading pretty good from afoot or horseback.

The next summer, Snowball went up to the Tin Cup Range with the yearling heifers. Snowball got to know the country, and the heifers started following Snowball and the music he carried with him. That fall he didn't know any more about the trail coming this way than the heifers did. But he has learned a lot since. Snowball is an asset to the ranch. I suppose they'll retire him someday.

That day I thought I had better move off the trail and let

the herd go by. Snowball traveled in the lead with the herd of faithful heifers following behind. The confident steer never looked back. Snowball walked along, carrying himself with all the dignity his responsible position called for.

"Howdy, Mr. Mark," a voice called. It was Henry, riding along behind the first thirty yearlings.

"Howdy, Mr. Henry," I replied. "The heifers look good."

Up ahead I could see Snowball sniffing the trail my horse had made through the snow. He would take the herd home. I moved over to ride with Henry and to get the latest news of the ranch.

Henry was riding Bingo, a tall, chestnut thoroughbred. Going back through the years, I wouldn't want to guess how many cows Henry and Bingo had chased together. Bingo was Henry's favorite horse. More than that, the tall horse was an important part of Henry's life.

I gave Bingo an admiring glance. "You know, Henry, if anything happens to that horse, they might as well shoot you."

Henry laughed. "That's about right, Mark." Henry rubbed the white stubble of whiskers on his chin, and his face sobered. I regretted making that comment.

Henry is a product of the western country in which he lives. His family homesteaded not far from our area before the turn of the century. Henry rode a horse to country school and was never absent one day. He started working at the cowboy trade early in his life and has been a man on a horse ever since.

The trail twisted through pine forest much of the time. Here and there, small open draws crossed the trail, inviting the yearlings to go that way. Once in awhile, we put a few adventurous heifers back on track. But in general, it was an easy drive. Henry and I continued to visit. When we topped a divide, I looked back and waved to the two young fellows who were bringing the rest of the yearlings along without any problems.

About mid-afternoon, we counted the heifers through the gate and dropped them along Jawbone Creek. The riders stopped for coffee and to say hello to Mary, then headed down the trail.

ø ø ø

Each fall Mary and I try to hang up some winter meat. Winter meat around here means an elk. We probably see as many elk during the summer as anyone in this part of the Rocky Mountains. That comes about, I think, because these local elk have accepted us as part of the environment in which they live. But all that changes in the fall.

About the time frost starts coating the grass each night and the aspen leaves turn yellow, elk camps start showing up along the little creeks. Pack strings come and go. Coleman lanterns make bright lights here and there. The various sounds of camp chores being done echo off the hillsides. And finally, man-scent wafts up from the sheltered draws and rides the air currents along the ridges. That's when the elk become man-shy. And they are shy of this man, too.

I hardly ever hunt during the early part of the season. Hanging up wild meat too soon could mean we might lose it from spoiling if the weather turned warm. Sometimes I wait too long. By the time the weather stays cold, the end of the season is looking me in the eye. I have to hunt long, hard and constant to get an elk.

One year I hunted faithfully for winter meat on what might be called my home range. Seems as if I walked a thousand miles and never got a shot at an elk.

In desperation, I rode back into that jungle we call Doomsday Creek. I got an elk all right. A good one. A young bull. And I earned every pound of that elk meat.

After I had dressed out the elk, it took me two hours to reach any kind of a trail. I walked and led my horse down narrow draws where sapling-size aspen grew so thick I had to stop often and back up, searching for a way through. Once I got rimrocked and had to find another way around. Crossing some of those swamps, I had to step high and quick to keep from bogging down. But my horse sank deep. Every time he pulled a hoof out, it made a loud whooshing noise. I was concerned he might have a shoe sucked right off.

Hours later, I was glad to see the light from the Coleman lantern Mary had hung outside.

I went back the next day with a couple of pack horses to get the meat. I won't go into the details, but like I said, I earned every pound of it.

Whenever I ride into camp with each of two pack horses loaded with a quarter of elk on a side, Mary is there waiting, ready to go to work. She has a bucket of clean water handy, dry towels, white cloth meat covers, two or three knives and the steel to sharpen them with. And you can bet the two dogs and the cat are close by, each ready for a handout.

We hang each quarter of elk from our meat pole which is well overhead. The pole spans the distance between the two trees that support it. When each quarter is raised by a rope to the height of the pole, it is out of the reach of dogs and coyotes. We just hope the dogs will keep a bear on the move.

But first, each quarter of meat must be trimmed and cleaned. One quarter will also be skinned. For that job, the meat is lowered to handy working height. I can think back to the days when I, the mighty hunter, used to do all that. But things have changed. Nowadays, Mary prefers to do that work herself.

I remember the first year Mary took over on that chore. Of course, I taught her everything she knows about the job. I thought it only proper I stand by, in case she wanted any advice. Looking over Mary's shoulder, I watched her work.

She handled that big butcher knife as though she was attacking something. "Her fingers! She'll cut them off!" I thought. I tried to keep calm.

"Mary, Sweetheart," I stammered. "Would you like me to give you a hand with that?"

"No thanks, Honey," Mary answered. "You go ahead. I know you have lots to do."

I stuck around. There was no way I could go off and leave her by herself. Mary shifted her position so I couldn't see good. I shifted mine so I could see better. Mary was pretty quiet. She wasn't smiling like she usually does. I could see she wasn't doing it the way I taught her. Mary shouldn't use that big knife. She should use the other one. The one with the black handle. I picked up the black-handled knife and stepped forward to show Mary how it should be done. That was a mistake.

I found Mary's big butcher knife waving under my nose. Her eyes were half-closed, but I could see the blazing fire within. Her lips were drawn tight across her teeth. I don't think she meant to be smiling.

"Honey," she said. (I was glad she still called me Honey.) "You keep your cotton-pickin' hands off this meat, or there is going to be one less mouth to feed around here this winter."

I backed up a couple of steps. I know my nose is long, but I didn't want to lose any of it.

"Now, Sweetheart, don't get your feathers ruffled," I said. "I was just trying to help."

Mary advanced another step. She was still waving that big, long knife under my nose. "Git," she said.

I backed up. I felt something under my foot. The cat squalled, then tried to bite my leg. My feet tangled, and down I fell. Tasha chased Maggie up a tree. Skipper licked my face and whined. From flat on my back, I looked up at Mary. She was laughing so hard tears ran down her cheeks.

Well, anyhow, when I bring home an elk, Mary cleans and trims three quarters, but leaves the hide on. Each piece has the exposed side covered with a clean, white cloth, and that is secured by twine. A canvas tarp is wrapped around each quarter, and a light Manila rope holds it in place. The tarp is used to keep gray jays, Clark's nutcrackers, and chickadees from pecking on the meat. Those three quarters are hoisted aloft and allowed to freeze.

The quarter that has been skinned is then cut into handy pieces ready to cook. Those cuts are wrapped in freezer paper and stored outside in a metal container until they freeze. They are then put in our meat cache on the north side of the cabin. That meat is what we will use as we go into the winter.

The meat cache has top, bottom, and sides made of sawdust-filled, nine-inch walls. The cache is ten cubic feet inside and is filled with sawdust. Access is through a lift-out door in the top. The cache has been used to keep some stuff frozen. And at other times, to keep some food from freezing.

Now about those three quarters of elk still hanging from our meat pole. It soon freezes hard. Then it is taken down. The canvas tarp is removed and is replaced by a tight-fitting plastic wrap. Each quarter is placed in an empty thirty-gallon metal drum. We set the drum under an Engelmann spruce where the sun never gets to it. We pack snow around each quarter of meat and then fit a metal cover on the drum.. The snow settles, then becomes almost as hard as ice. We add more snow as necessary during the winter. Drain holes in the bottom of the drum let melted snow run out. We leave the hide on the quarter to prevent too much moisture loss due to dehydration.

Whenever we need more meat, Mary takes a quarter out, skins it, and cuts it up as before. We have been able to keep meat fresh right up to Easter. I might add that before cooking it, Mary always soaks wild meat in a saltwater solution for twenty-four hours. She smokes some pieces by using Liquid Smoke. Some meat is put by for summer use by canning it under pressure in her pressure cooker.

Some people have asked why we don't just let the meat hang from the meat pole after it is frozen hard. Well, even in our coldest winters, there are times when we have a warm spell that lasts longer than is good for keeping meat frozen hard. The risk of losing meat from spoilage is too great to leave it hanging.

Ø Ø Ø

The days of late fall move along. It snows more often, and morning temperatures are often zero or lower. The cattle still left on the mountain work the lower parts of the range. There, the snow doesn't build up as deep when the storms do come. And later when the sun comes out, the lower country is the first to bare off. But there is only so much lower country, with only so much cured grass left for the cattle grazing there. I ride down that way. The signs of the range and the look of the cattle tell me it is time to take them home.

A couple of days later, riders from the ranch move in at the cow camp just before dark. They turn their horses out below the cabin. Someone fires up the old Monarch stove. Supper is cooked and coffee is brewed. Tall tales are told. Old hands bed down on the plank bunks. Young bucks roll out on the floor and hope that the mice that use the place for a steeple chase course won't keep them awake all night.

The next morning under dirty-gray skies, the riders split up, and each man rides to the head of a draw. If the draw is wide, two riders may be used for the sweep.

On some high-up vantage point, riders get off, snug up a cinch, and scan the country below. Climbing aboard, they give out with a whoop and a holler, each in his own style.

Cows and calves lift their heads and look around, then move down the draw together. The five pairs ahead fall in with six pairs from another draw. Joined up, they move down the branch of a creek toward its fork.

The cattle are not hard to move. They know the signs and sounds of a late fall gather. Small bunches merge to make big bunches, and they all get together to make a herd. Old Crooked-horn takes the lead, and down the trail they go.

One year I found myself riding along with Ol' Zeke during the fall roundup. I was glad for the chance to visit. Zeke has a spread of his own to run, but takes time to help neighbors at a branding or to get cattle off in the fall.

Zeke is another product of this western land he loves. As a pistol kid, his dad rode a horse alongside the covered wagon his grandfather drove into this country.

Ol' Zeke grew up chasing cows and has been doing that most of the time ever since. I doubt he would want to do anything else. The farthest he ever got away from a horse was to pack mules for the U.S. Army. And a mule is half horse.

Ol' Zeke is sort of an ornery cuss at times. But put all together, he is a good fellow. A staunch friend. And a top hand, afoot or on horseback.

That afternoon we both reined in our horses and watched the herd below us string out. The old cowboy shoved his big hat back and scratched where his hair should be.

"They're goin' to go, Mark," Zeke said. He stuck out a big paw and we shook. "Stop by whenever you're down, Mark."

"Thanks, Zeke. I'll do that."

Zeke rode off and let his horse pick his way down the hill. I waved to the other riders along the slope, then turned my horse toward the skyline far above.

As my horse climbed and rested on that long haul home,

I got to thinking about Alkali Rob and the time he rode into camp one day last summer. Over coffee cups, we got to reminiscing about some years long past. Rob told me about a trip he made to the mountains with Zeke early one fall.

It seems they were headed for the Wolf Track cow camp to gather some cattle. The extra horse they each led carried their bedrolls and the grub they would need for a few days' stay on the mountain.

The trail was good, and the climb toward the camp was not hard. It was a little dry, perhaps. But beyond that, Rob and Zeke had good reason to be enjoying the crisp fall day.

Ol' Zeke rode a bronc called Spud. He was a four-year-old at the time. I remember him well. He was a well-made sorrel with a blaze face. And he was as waspy as all get out.

Those two good hands rode at a sensible pace and told tall tales as they did. Mostly, Zeke told Rob about his days in the Tenth Mountain Division. That must have been quite an outfit, and Zeke has a lot of good stories to tell.

Their horses heard the sounds first. "Baa, baa, baa." The four horses stopped in their tracks, heads up, ears pricked forward. Moving under a cloud of brown dust, a whole band of sheep came down the trail. A thousand sheep. And every one saying, "Baa." Not once, but continually. Those four horses, all pretty young, had heard plenty of cows say, "Moo." But they didn't know a darn thing about a sheep that says, "Baa." Those woolly sheep looked different and smelled different. The four young horses were terrified.

In a couple of seconds, Zeke and Rob had their hands full. Rob managed to get well off the trail with his horses and found safer ground behind a big rock. Out in the middle of the trail, Zeke had problems. Spud was white-eyed with fear and wanted to quit the country. The pack horse Zeke led wasn't doing any better. That kept Zeke from handling the bronc like

he should. The pack horse ran around behind Spud. His lead rope ran up under the gelding's tail. Spud clamped down hard, and the rope was held fast.

Spud let out a squall. He bogged his head and started to buck. The bronc was as quick as a cat, twisting this way and that, in stiff-legged, pile-driving jolts. A horse that bucks was no stranger to Zeke. Broncs had been a part of his life. But that wasn't Zeke's day to ride. With his nose down close to his front feet, Spud spun to the right. Zeke became unglued. Spread-eagled, he took flight, then landed in the dust.

The noisy, crowding sheep filled the trail. Those in the lead balked for a moment at seeing Zeke's stretched-out body lying in the dust. Some shied and went around. Most jumped across Zeke as easy as they would clear a log lying across a mountain trail.

Zeke lay belly down, his hands folded across his head. The surging tide of sheep kept coming. The dust became thick, and the characteristic odor of sheep became heavier. Those sheep were an agile bunch. Rob had to admire the easy grace with which they sailed across Zeke's flaked-out body.

Finally, the entire band of sheep passed by, as did their herder a minute later. Alkali Rob caught Zeke's horses, which never got very far away from his own. Zeke got to his feet. He picked up his hat and looked at it with disgust. He beat it several times against his pant leg trying to get the dust off. The best he could, Zeke put it back into shape and plunked it on his head. Mostly, he blew his nose and kept spitting repeatedly as if he had a bad taste in his mouth.

Rob brought Zeke's horses over. Zeke nodded his thanks. The cowboy wasn't hurt. He was humiliated. Without uttering a word, he mounted and started the sorrel gelding up the trail.

Ol' Zeke has been kind of touchy about sheep ever since.

 Casey

THE SOUNDS OF WIND-DRIVEN snow beating against the window panes roused me out of a fitful sleep. Close to the cabin, tall lodgepole pines swayed in the wind and made eerie noises in the night.

By rights, I should have been sleeping soundly. I was tired enough. I had spent the day riding up one draw and down the other, through a foot of fresh snow looking for half-dozen yearling heifers that came up missing from the fall gather. The chill mantle of dusk was wrapping around me by the time I found the yearlings and moved them in with three cow-calf pairs who knew the way down the trail toward home.

Tossing and turning in my warm bed, I listened to the sounds of the storm and thought back through the years to another fall and to memories of a special horse I called Casey. One of those experiences haunts me even now.

Casey came into my life when Mary and I were still living down at the Deer Creek Ranch. I noticed him first when he was running at the side of his mother in the brood mare bunch. Seemingly without effort, the brown colt stayed shoulder to shoulder with the mare as she galloped and turned with the herd on one of their wild, free runs.

One hot day, I came upon the mares and foals shaded-up in a grove of aspen, close up to the face of the mountain. I eased my saddle horse around looking for the colt I had already named Casey. He was easy to find because he stood out in a class of his own.

Curiosity brought Casey forward to look us over. The leggy brown colt stood four-square, ears pricked forward as he sized up the horse I was riding. My saddle horse bobbed his head violently and sneezed to chase away annoying nose flies. The movement spooked Casey. He whirled around and trotted back to join his mother as the band of horses moved farther back in the grove of aspen. I turned my horse and rode away.

Heading for home that late forenoon, I did some thinking about Casey. During our brief visit, I noticed scabbed-over wounds above Casey's right eye. I was curious. Later, I talked to my friend and neighbor, Alkali Rob, who took care of the brood mares. He always had a thought about such things. Rob said he figured the colt got hurt when his mother was being remated not long after she foaled. Rob's thinking seemed logical enough. I thought no more about the scabbed-over wounds above Casey's right eye.

The next summer, whenever I had the time, I rode out of my way to see how Casey was doing with the yearlings. Those youngsters continued to grow after weaning as they had been grained good when Rob had them in for halter breaking and gentling. Now, with the green grass of the foothills loaded with the nutrients they needed, they would grow some more.

When I pulled up my horse, the yearlings came around for a visit. After a while they found some excuse to spook. Off they went at a gallop. Casey always led the pack, tail flying like a banner, his forefeet well out in front. The message came back to me that I was watching a colt who loved life and planned on living it to the fullest. Then and there, I knew I wanted Casey in my string someday.

As a green-broke, gangling three-year-old, Casey did

come my way. The first day I rode him he put me to the test. Casey really never bucked, but he sure had me thinking he might come uncorked any minute. I rode the brown colt three days in a row. Those up-and-down miles along the face of the mountain can sure change a bronc's mind about some things. At the end of the three days, Casey and I had reached an understanding of mutual benefit.

One year moved into the next. Casey got some size. His deep heart girth made a place for lungs of vast capacity, and he had lots of daylight under his belly. Casey developed into a light-mouthed, easy-reining horse. He watched a cow with real interest, and it took a pretty agile critter to get away from him.

By the time Casey reached five, his right eye had turned opaque, but he still flinched when I flicked a finger at him. I thought back to what Alkali Rob told me about what might have happened when Casey was a very young foal.

Casey was the horse I saddled when I had a big, outside circle to ride. The brown horse was physically and temperamentally suited for the job. I can remember some of those early morning roundups on a branding day in May. Meadowlark music and the smell of lupine were a couple things that made getting up before daylight worthwhile. Another thing that made it worthwhile was the feel of a good horse under you— a horse that was enjoying the morning and the work as much as you. Casey was that kind of a horse.

I recall vividly the sense of partnership I felt with Casey when I stopped him on some high point to take in the movement of the cattle below. It wasn't just me who watched and listened to the cows and calves stringing down the draw. Head moving from side to side, ears pricked forward, Casey took a real interest, too.

Casey wasn't the so-called ideal horse. For instance, at calving time he wasn't the best horse to use. At times, a rider has to move a cow with her new calf from one place to another. The slow pace of the job frustrated Casey. It wasn't long before he shook his head and pranced in place. I was concerned he would step on the calf.

Another thing. As time went on, Casey got pretty touchy about movements on his right side, from people or other animals. Finally the day came when I flicked my hand at Casey's right eye. The brown horse never flinched. He had no sight in that eye. Casey was a one-eyed horse.

Casey never thought much of the idea of having iron shoes nailed to his feet. But, Anvil, our horseshoer, was a man of much horse savvy. I always felt Anvil had forgotten more about a horse than I would ever know. Anvil always worked slow and careful with Casey. Through the years, he got the job done without trouble.

Then one day after we determined Casey was completely blind on his right side, I watched Anvil set a hind foot down after the final dressing with a rasp. Anvil stretched to get the kink out of his back. Walking forward, he patted Casey on the neck as if to say thank you. Turning, Anvil looked at me steady in the eye. "Mark, more than ever now, this is one horse I don't want to have a fight with."

I nodded my agreement. "Yup, he's a one-eyed horse now."

Anvil continued to fix his eyes on mine. "Mark, he isn't just a one-eyed horse. Casey is a one-man horse. Yours. I know. I've been watching you and Casey for quite awhile."

As time went along, Casey became more suspicious of most people. As that feeling grew, it became more apparent his trust in me was getting firmer. I guess some people would say our relationship was based on the acceptance of imperfections. I took Casey with all his imperfections. Casey took me with all my imperfections.

When Mary and I left Deer Creek Ranch and moved up to the cow camp in the high country, Casey came along. His lungs did a good job of pumping this thin air. And his prominent withers held my saddle in place without me having to cinch it up too tight.

Casey adjusted to seeing life through one eye. Riding Casey down treacherous mountain trails never caused me concern because the brown horse kept his mind on the job. Casey put his nose down close to the trail so his one good eye did the job of two.

In the course of moving cattle up one hill and down the other, Casey and I shared a lot of mountain country. Riding along, I shared a lot of private thoughts with Casey, too. Ol' Case moved his ears back and forth like he was taking it all in. They say a friend should be a good listener. Casey qualified very well on that score.

At the end of a warm day in late summer, I pulled my saddle off Casey. The horse was ganted up more than the work of one day should have caused. Casey needed some rest. I turned him out to run free and fill up on good mountain grass. Casey would listen for the bell on one of the horses running loose. By morning, he would be joined up with the bunch and have company.

The next afternoon, I was riding toward home when I came across the loose horses stringing up out of an aspen draw where they had shaded-up during the middle of the day. I looked the horses over as they topped out on a hard-grass flat. Casey wasn't with them. Then below me in the draw, I heard a horse nicker. It was Casey. He hobbled along on three legs trying to catch up with the bunch.

I rode down the hill to meet the brown horse. Casey waited for me. I found what any horseman hates to see. Since I turned Casey out, only twenty-four hours earlier, the horse had gotten badly cut by barbed wire on his right front foot—his blind side.

To this day, I don't know for sure where Casey got in trouble. A wild guess would be to say my one-eyed horse tangled with some barbed wire hiding in the sagebrush, the remnants of a fence around an old grazing homestead.

I used my lariat to make a halter so I could lead Casey back to camp. Traveling mostly on three legs, the horse played out easily. It was a slow trip home.

Back at the camp, I found the stuff in my vet kit which I needed to produce a local anesthetic at the wound. I cleaned the jagged cut which was of considerable length and depth. Then, the best I could, I pulled the lips of the wound together with surgical thread. I spent the rest of the summer treating the wound with medicine almost daily. Before it came time to turn Casey out for the winter his foot had healed, and he traveled without limping.

The next spring I got Casey shod as usual. It was great to be aboard the brown horse again. His step was springy, and he seemed to have as much endurance as ever. That was early in the season. By midsummer, a change showed in Casey's way of going. In the middle of the afternoon, he would start to favor his right front foot. Casey was hurting. Anvil reshod him with a three-quarter shoe. It helped some, but not enough.

I turned Casey out. A good rest is all he needs, I hoped. A month later, I saw him traveling along with the loose horses. Casey seemed to be moving as good as the rest of the bunch. I took him back to camp with me.

The next morning I saddled Casey and used him on a short, easy ride. When the horse had to carry the weight of a rider, he favored that right front foot as before. Regretfully, I faced the reality of the situation, as have many other riders before me. It meant the end of a working partnership where

shared adventures were part of the day. Scar tissue was causing poor circulation in Casey's right front foot. Arthritis had
set in. It was very unlikely the horse would ever be sound
again. I pulled Casey's shoes and turned him out, never to
toss a saddle on him again.

Casey wintered down in the foothills and came back up
the next spring with the rest of our string. Casey wasn't
wearing shoes. As a pensioner, he wouldn't need them. All
the brown horse had to do was to drink cool mountain water,
fill himself with lush grass, and enjoy the view of the majes-
tic, tall peaks. I considered it little enough thanks for what he
had given me.

Casey got fat on a regimen like that. In company with
other loose horses, he drifted past the camp every few days.
Casey was usually the first to put his head over the gate looking for a handout of grain cake. It wasn't that he needed the
extra feed. Casey just needed to be shown he was still part of
our horse family, even though he wasn't working in his turn
as he used to.

Many times I studied Casey's way-of-going when he
drifted by camp. I was often tempted to saddle him and take a
short ride. Just for old time's sake. But I knew it wouldn't be
the thing to do. Casey wouldn't feel the same under me. It
would just remind me that the Casey I had known in the past
was gone. And he wouldn't be coming back.

Fall moved in early that year with snow and cold temperatures. The cattle were gathered and moved out of the high
country. Soon after, elk hunters pulled their camps and went
on down the trail. As far as we knew, Mary and I were the
only people on the mountain.

The horses grew winter hair and drifted by for a handout
more often. Casey was no longer the first to put his head over
the gate. He was in the drag, stiff and clumsy on the front end.

But his condition was still pretty good because of the fat he laid on during the summer.

With the last of our winter supplies packed in, it was time to take our horses down to Deer Creek to be turned loose in the foothills until the grass showed green and strong in the spring. Where did Casey fit in that plan?

Then without much warning, the weather became harsher. Casey lost flesh and drew up in the flanks. Casey was hurting. And I hurt with him. I put Casey in the corral and fed him a good ration of grain cake and hay cubes. That treatment didn't fit Casey's temperament. The brown horse gimped along the fence, whinnying and looking in the direction where he knew his herdmates roamed free.

I turned Casey out. The best he could, he followed in the wake of the other horses as they worked the south slopes, pawing through the snow for cured grass.

Then I had a dream. A dream that reached the bottom of the barrel of my emotions and honed my nerves to a raw edge. I woke up cold and shivering, recalling the scenario I heard and saw in my dream. I saw our horses galloping freely, just after sunset, through fresh snow that billowed up behind them.

It was a happy scene—until in the drag I saw Casey. He was whinnying to the other horses, begging them to wait for him as he tried in vain to keep up.

The other horses galloped over a divide and disappeared from Casey's sight. Casey pulled up, but continued to whinny. By now, the rest of the bunch was too far away to hear his pleading call.

Vividly in the dream, I saw Casey's head settle lower in front of his chest. Finally his silhouette became unclear in the gathering darkness. On a hilltop, not far away, a family of coyotes sent their lupine calls into the brittle, oncoming night.

The next day when I saw Casey crippling along behind

the other horses, I lashed out at him. For the moment, I was emptied of sympathy. I lashed out at Casey for not staying sound forever. Then I brought my wrath down on the mare or stud who kicked him in the head when he was a new foal. I cussed the company who made the barbed wire and the homesteader who left it lying in the sagebrush. In frustration, I berated myself up one side and down the other because I couldn't help the brown horse who watched me with one trusting eye.

That night as I lay in bed, I wasn't in turmoil as I had been for many days. After weighing all the considerations, I had made a decision that affected the life of the horse I called Casey and my own life as well. Because I didn't have a road and horse trailer to use to get Casey off the mountain, whatever I did to help the horse would have to be done right up here in the high country.

Outside, I could hear two horses pawing in the snow, searching out the last of the hay cubes I had strung out before dark. Casey and Kyska fed nose to nose. They were close friends of long standing. Tonight was a good time for Casey to have Kyska around. Later when the night got cold, they stood close together in the lee of an Englemann spruce, glad of each other's company.

When morning finally came, I went out and found the two. I put a halter on Casey and led him to the hitch rail where I had saddled him so many times in the past. The brown horse walked right up with slack in the lead rope. The night before I had given Casey a heavy dose of Butazolidin. For a short while, Casey wouldn't be feeling his usual pain.

Kyska had followed along. I tied him close-by and saddled him.

I fed both horses a special breakfast. Not their usual hard horse cake. Some time past, a friend had left a sack of oats rolled in molasses. That's what Casey and Kyska got. I almost always divvy up even when I feed. This time I put a little extra in Casey's feedpan.

As Casey chomped on rolled oats and molasses, I brushed him as if he was going to a horse show. His mane and tail had a few burrs. I picked them out then used the Scotch comb to get rid of the tangles.

I walked into the house to eat my own breakfast. A cup of coffee was all I wanted. Mary and I didn't do much talking. It wasn't the first time Mary saw me having to face up to the responsibility of an unpleasant but necessary job.

I took the 30-30 off its pegs and went back out. There, I shoved the carbine into the scabbard strapped to my saddle. Both our dogs disappeared under the cabin. They seemed to have a premonition that they would be asked to stay home that morning.

With Casey's lead rope in hand, I swung aboard Kyska and rode past the cabin. When I ride away, Mary always comes out on the porch to say good-bye to me one more time. That morning she stayed inside.

I rode slowly. I had a special place to go to, but I didn't want to get there any sooner than I had to. It was a quiet ride. I wasn't talking to myself or the horses like I usually do.

Finally, I came to a small open draw surrounded by tall granite crags and scattered Douglas fir. It was a place where Casey and I had eaten our lunch many times.

I dismounted and tied up Kyska. Carbine in hand, I led Casey farther down the draw. I was trying not to think of the job I had to do. For a few moments, I wanted to be a mechanical man—a man without feelings.

I tied up Casey. I spoke not a word nor touched him with my hand.

I stepped back and raised the 30-30. Casey turned my

way. One eye cloudy, unseeing. The other eye questioning.

Conflicting thoughts raced through my mind.

He has a right to live.

He has a right to die.

The bead of the front sight held steady on a small, white star on Casey's forehead.

Roughly, coldly, I shoved emotion aside. I sucked in my breath and squeezed the trigger. The silence of the draw was shattered by the sound of the one shot.

The brown horse dropped in his tracks, drained of life in an instant. Casey would never suffer pain again.

My last words to Casey are too private to share with even you, my friend, with whom I've shared some private thoughts.

I turned and made my way toward my saddle horse. Half blinded. Staggering.

I shoved the carbine in the scabbard and mounted. I rode away—and I never looked back.

A Full Cache

THE SEASON MOVED ALONG. Midday temperatures were high enough to melt the snow along the rimrocks facing south. But after the sun dipped below the sawtooth ridge of Cougar Mountain, a forewarning chill moved in. It was typical to have the thermometer on the porch tell us it was close to zero by the time the black mantle of night settled on the high country.

Just before dark, Mary returned from her last trip to the low country. That final trip to town is an important one for Mary. Among other things, that is when she sends off Christmas packages to our children and grandchildren. Grandchildren. Amazing. First you have one. Next thing you know, you have something akin to a co-ed scout troop. They are nice to have.

Then, too, there is the matter of eggs. Mary's final trip to town is when she buys all the eggs we will use through the winter and until June of the next year. She usually gets forty-five dozen. They weigh about seventy-five pounds boxed. Before she left, I suggested she take only one pack horse, as, certainly, one horse could pack the eggs. I had to make another trip down anyhow. Mary came back, "Don't be silly. That would be like putting all my eggs in one basket. Besides, I'm a two-pack-horse woman. You needn't try to cut me down."

Many people ask how we manage to keep eggs from

185

going bad over that length of time. I can tell you how Mary handles the eggs. She buys the best eggs available in the store. Within a few hours, she has greased each egg with a solid shortening such as Crisco. That seals off the pores in the shell so no air can enter to act on the yolk and the white. Mary has tried using an oil for the job, but that doesn't work as well. As she works, she wraps each egg in tissue paper and returns it to the egg carton, small end down. That keeps the air cell within the shell in its normal position at the big end of the egg.

After the eggs get on the mountain, they must be stored where it is cool, but where they won't freeze. Mary stores the eggs in about four different places. (Again, she doesn't want to put them "all in one basket.") Some eggs are stored underground. Others are placed within a big pile of pine needles, then covered with snow. Some are stored in our meat cache. Mary always puts several dozen eggs in the side storeroom. In every case, she places the egg cartons within a cardboard box and fills the empty spaces in the box with sawdust. Whatever the situation may be, insulation is the key to keeping eggs cool in warm weather and keeping them from freezing in cold weather.

In a recent winter we had fifty-four days of below-zero weather. We had two days of thirty-three below zero. Mary found ten frozen eggs. In such a case, Mary leaves them frozen until she wants to use them. (Frozen potatoes can be handled the same way.) Through the years, we have found only a couple of eggs that were not fresh in June.

I asked Mary to jot down the amounts of some of the supplies we have on hand at the start of our six or seven months of snowed-in winter. This is nowhere near a complete list of all of our supplies. Here is Mary's list:

100 lbs. flour
100 lbs. sugar

50 lbs. brown sugar (for making syrup)
30 lbs. oleo
30 lbs. canned bacon
45 dozen eggs
8 8-ounce jars instant coffee
15 lbs. perk coffee
8 4-ounce jars of powdered tea
18 lbs. shortening
30 lbs. honey
30 lbs. powdered milk
20 lbs. mashed potato flakes
5 lbs. dried sliced potatoes
50 lbs. fresh potatoes
50 lbs. fresh apples

In the summer, Mary dries all kinds of vegetables and apples on the grill around our stove. She dries the leaves of wild strawberry, raspberry, fireweed and mint. They make a pretty good tea.

About storage: we have three built-on storerooms. Before I go any further, I want to tell you that on these projects we used what some people refer to as the Scandinavian concept of laying up logs. Briefly, a vee is cut in the bottom of all logs, the full length of the log. Insulation is laid, full length, in the vee. The insulation is held in place by masking tape. The next log being laid fits on the bottom log like a saddle fits a horse. No chinking is needed. With hindsight, we wish we had done all our building that way.

I might mention that for one of those storerooms, we made all the lumber used for floor, door, roof and shelves with our chain saw and lumber-making attachment.

ø ø ø

Mary was atop the mountain for the winter. She wouldn't be making another trip to town until spring. That wasn't so in my case. I still had to make one trip off the mountain to purchase supplies I refer to as "shop stuff."

So a few days later found me at the Deer Creek Place. I spent some time visiting with the crew there before they rode off for the project of the morning. Returning to the storeroom, I sorted the supplies I had purchased the day before in town.

Among other things, I'd bought all the nuts and bolts, nails and spikes that I thought I would need for the construction jobs of the winter. I have found galvanized flashing handy to have around. So I bought a roll. We had planned another skylight and needed two pieces of quarter-inch plexiglass for the double-paned light, along with some two-by-eight inch fir for the crib.

I'd purchased gas and oil for the chain saw and kerosene for our lamps. Stove oil was needed to mix with PENTA and creosote for preserving and staining any log or pole work I might do.

As I did each fall, I brought down our chain saw and took it to the shop where I bought it several years ago. There, they took it apart and replaced worn parts as needed. My thought was to prevent trouble from happening. It seemed to pay off. The chain saw was ready to go home.

This trip was our last chance for fresh vegetables and fruit. Mary had given me a list, and I had the box packed and ready to go. Last but not least, we had received enough mail and early Christmas packages to almost make a load for one pack horse.

All the stuff was weighed and stacked in organized piles down the center of the saddleroom floor. Each pile represented the cargo that would go on one horse. All I needed were the horses. I hustled out to get them.

They were waiting near the gate when I got to the horse pasture. I put a halter on my saddle horse and led him in, with the other four following along behind. In front of the saddle-room, I strung out some horse cake on the grass. About that time, a pickup bumped across the cattle guard, then came to a stop in front of the old shop. Sam stepped out.

"By gosh, Mark, I was just going by and saw you bringing in your horses, so I said to myself, 'By gosh, I'll just go in there and hold a horse for old Mark'."

"Well, golly, Sam, I'm sure glad you stopped. I can use a horse holder this morning. I'm running late."

I've known Sam for thirty years. He had spent most of his life chasing cows in the foothills and leading pack strings along dim trails in the mountains. Sam has been doing it differently lately. He and his wife spend their summers at a high mountain lake. There, Sam controls the amount of water that goes out through the headgate to fill irrigation ditches in the low country. In the winter, Sam makes custom horse gear in the good shop he has at his home in town.

Nobody ever called Sam tall and lanky. Now white-bearded and pink-skinned, he usually wears a warm smile and has a ready laugh that makes his face light up like a jolly Santa Claus.

As it turned out, Sam did a lot more than hold horses that morning. He pitched right in currying and brushing the horses I haltered and tied up to the corral fence. When he had a horse ready, he led it to the hitch rail. There, I tossed on pads and saddle. Sam, on the other side, straightened out straps and passed cinches back under to me. Sam worked with the confidence that comes from long experience. The horses were comfortable with the man.

Later, we packed the horses as a team. Sam on the off side. Myself on the near. Sam enjoyed himself. "Gosh, Mark," he said. "I'm glad I stopped by. You couldn't have got 'em packed by yourself." His eyes twinkled, and he laughed out loud. Sam examined each outfit with interest. Full of enthusiasm, he said, "Yes sir, I like the way you have that fixed," or, "By gosh, that's a good idea, Mark." We spread a tarp over each load, then straightened it until it set just right. Then we threw and tightened double diamonds.

I put on my chaps and heavy coat. Sam looked over each horse and pack, loosening a strap here, tightening a strap there. He had done it many times before.

I bridled my saddle horse and snugged up his cinch. Sam lined up the four pack horses and made them ready for the trail. Sam was impressed with the manners of our horses.

I got mounted, and Sam handed up the lead rope of the first horse in the string. Sam wasn't through helping yet. With an enthusiastic hustle, he went ahead to open the gate.

Sam watched the outfit come his way. I could see his eyes appraise each horse in the string. He nodded his approval. "Packs look good, Mark. And, by gosh, you've got the best horses in the whole darn country."

I pulled up and shook Sam's hand. "Thanks, Sam, for all your help."

Sam's face was still full of sunshine. "My thanks to you, Mark. I can't think of anything I would rather do on my seventy-fifth birthday than help you get started for the mountain."

I lifted my reins and rode on. Going up a little hill, I turned and looked back along the string of lined-up pack horses. Down by the gate, Sam smiled and waved. I had good reason to smile, too. I was glad Santa Claus had come a bit early in the year.

Adios

"**Y**OU AND MARY have a good winter."

"If you run out of Coleman fuel, Mark, just go down to my camp and help yourself. You know where I cache it."

"Here, Mark, take this bacon home to Mary. I'll be darned if I'm going to pack it off."

That's the way the talk went that afternoon at the old cow camp. I was there gathering some horses when the last of the elk camps was moving off the mountain. The people and animals from two camps were going off together. Some of those fellows packed elk. A few had hunted hard and long and still were unsuccessful in their quest for the wily wapiti. Successful or not, they very likely enjoyed their stay on the mountain.

I wished those rancher-neighbor types a mild winter so they wouldn't run out of hay. And a Merry Christmas, too. With a wave of a hand, they rode off with pack mules and pack horses strung out behind. I watched until they disappeared around a bend in the trail.

A light but restless wind came up, hazing goose-down snowflakes this way and that. Finally the white flakes settled and built up in the tracks just made in the packed snow.

ø ø ø

Back home, it was almost dark before I got around to doing evening chores. I strung out grain cake in the lee of

some Engelmann spruce and followed it up with bright green hay cubes. The horses fussed a bit then lined up in their recognized peck order.

Heading for the house, I looked up through holes in the cloud cover to see yellow stars showing bright against a black velvet sky. A biting wind came in occasional gusts. It was going to be a night of on and off snow squalls with the temperature probably dipping below zero. That was about as bad as I wanted the weather to get for the next few days.

After supper, Mary and I enjoyed the warm comfort of the cabin that was to be our home for another winter of mountaintop solitude. The light from the hanging kerosene lamp cast soft shadows about the room, bringing out a golden tone on the aging logs. Close at Mary's feet, Tasha and Skipper lay stretched out on colorful Indian throw rugs. On Mary's lap, Maggie was fast asleep.

Mary's face held a look of contentment as she glanced around the room. The cook stove, with pots and pans hanging neatly behind it, held her eye. The oven wasn't big. But from it came an adequate supply of bread, rolls, cookies and pies to meet our needs.

The cupboards were of such a size and design as to make the best use of available space. The boards used in their construction came up the mountain as cargo on a couple of our dependable pack horses.

Mary gazed fondly at the shelves of books in the gable at the north end of the room. Some were books we had yet to read. Others were the kind one could read several times over in a lifetime and not tire of the thoughts therein.

Close at Mary's elbow was her own special bookshelf. It held her reference volumes on such subjects as spiritual philosophy, botany, and the bird and animal life of the high country.

I got up to put a stick of wood on the fire and to close the damper a bit. We weren't lacking for warmth.

Mary smiled her nice gentle smile when I returned to my chair. "Mark, it may not be big, but I like this cabin better than any home we've ever lived in."

I laughed. "I'm glad because this is where we are."

Then Mary went on. "But you know, on a night like this, I think of those poor people down there, worried about the water pipes freezing up or the power going off so the stoker furnace won't work."

I nodded. "Yup, I know what you mean. And tomorrow morning trying to start a vehicle."

"And putting tire chains on," Mary added. "I used to hate driving on those slippery roads."

"Worst of all is having a sewer line freeze up," I continued. "What a mess!"

Mary shook her head. "Those poor people. I feel so sorry for them."

From reports we got from time to time, we knew that as winter starts to close in, our friends down in the low country sooner or later got around to discussing "those two old people up on the mountain."

"Mary, the poor soul. I feel so sorry for her," someone might say. "Up on that mountain all winter with just him."

"Yes, and they say that their cabin is no bigger than our bathroom."

"Really! Speaking of bathrooms, I hear he makes her go outside," another probably adds.

"Really!"

"And do you know they have to carry water from the spring in a bucket."

"Yes, but I heard Mark widened the trail so Mary could carry two buckets at a time."

"Well, Mark always was an efficient cuss."

"I really shouldn't ask this. But what do you suppose they do about bathing?"

"I've often wondered about that myself. Mary, the poor soul."

"Well, you know what they say. It takes all kinds...."

I guess it might be summed up like this: they are happy to be down there with all their conveniences and miseries. And we are happy to be up here without their conveniences and miseries.

The quietness of the room was broken when both dogs dashed to the door barking and whining. Mary got up to let them out. Through the open cabin door, we could hear the yipping of coyotes below the cabin. The dogs disappeared into the dark. In a moment, they sent their lupine calls down the slope. In spite of the cold, Mary lingered at the door listening. After she closed it she spoke. But not about coyotes.

"Mark, the horses are really restless tonight."

"They know it's time."

"Yes, there's a time to bring them up and a time to take them down."

I nodded. I was glad to be taking them down in the morning. At Deer Creek, I would get their shoes pulled and their feet trimmed. The horses would get their annual worming. They would winter better if they did.

The last time I haltered each of them, I would use my jackknife to cut off his forelock. It would grow out by next June. In the meantime, burdock would not hang in that hair to flake off and get in their eyes.

With all that done, I would turn the horses loose to run free in the foothills, up close to the foot of the mountain. There they would have spring-fed streams to drink from, dry grass for feed, and sheltered draws to provide protection when sharp-fanged winds blew cold out of the north.

By daylight the next morning, only a few wispy snowflakes came down to settle on ten inches of new snow that built up during the night. Light and fluffy, it would not add much moisture to the soil. But it covered tracks and gave a fresh-laundered look to the mountain.

Right after breakfast, Mary and I went out to get the horses ready to go off the mountain. They drifted in as soon as they saw us stirring about. Our horses were easy to catch. Soon we had them haltered and tied up, and the horses turned-to on their grain. Mary curried and brushed and said something nice to each horse.

I removed the tarps covering the saddles on the long rack. Each tarp was given a shake to free it of snow, then folded and made ready to go off with the horses.

Mary and I have saddled so many horses together that we work well as a team. Working fast and without wasted motion, we soon had the string saddled and tied up in the order they would travel. Each pack horse carried all the gear he would need to bring up a light load next spring. We loaded mail as well as the snowshoes and packboard I would need for the trip back up the mountain.

I got into my chaps and put on my winter parka; then I tied an extra pair of gloves to my saddle. By then, Mary had opened the gate, had lined the horses up and had tied them together, head to tail.

I snugged up Bridger's cinch and turned him around. I found a low place for Bridger to stand and a high place for myself and climbed aboard. Mary handed me Nugget's lead rope and off I rode.

Bridger shook his head. He was eager to make tracks in the fresh snow. Going through the gate, I looked back along the string. Every horse was coming in a no-nonsense way. I

was proud of the horse I was riding and of the six strung out behind me.

Back at the gate, Mary stood with a dog on each side. Maggie perched on a gatepost. Mary smiled and waved good-bye. In a few more days, she would be there to welcome me home with the same warm smile.

Epilogue

SINCE THE LATE FALL DAY when I left Mary standing at the gate as I led our string of horses off the mountain, several changes have taken place in the lives of Mary and me. Because I have shared so many of our other experiences with you, I feel I want to share these, too.

The first change came about one day in early August of a later year. Mary was off the mountain purchasing winter supplies. I had some riding to do about seven miles from camp. The task was to straighten out a mix-up of cattle from adjacent ranges.

The job went well. By mid-afternoon, I was ready to point my horse toward home. About that time, big, black roiling clouds came sailing across the ridges from the east. Soon lightning flashed across the sky, and the sharp crack of thunder filled the narrow valley where I was.

I found shelter under a huge slab of rock that formed a shed big enough for my horse and me. There, I waited out what I considered the worst electrical storm I had experienced in all my years on the mountain. Lightning, thunder, rain and hail came in their turn, and at times, all together. Both my horse and I were relieved when it was over.

I rode home in the sunshine on water-washed trails. As I topped out on Agate Creek Divide, the strong smell of wood smoke reached my nose. I pulled up my horse and looked around. No telltale plume of smoke reached for the sky. Disturbed, I rode on.

As I neared home, the smell of wood smoke became stronger, and I put my horse into a trot. Going down the last hill, I called ahead to our two dogs. I had left them home as they would have been no help on the cattle sorting job of the day. Now they came to meet me, whining and trying to talk to me with their eyes.

I rounded the last bend in the trail and pulled up at the gate. I started to dismount, then stopped. Looking toward the cabin, I was brought up short in total disbelief and shock. Steam and smoke rose from the charred remains of our home of the past twelve years.

⌀ ⌀ ⌀

A few days later, I met Mary at the head of the Gunshot Trail. We talked in low tones as we discussed the fire. Staunch in spite of what happened, Mary offered her support to me.

I took charge of Mary's two pack horses, and we rode on to the old cow camp. We lived there the rest of the season. When the cattle went off the mountain that fall, we followed in a few days.

⌀ ⌀ ⌀

Living down in the low country took some adjusting on our part. The house we moved into on a large Black Angus ranch east of the mountains was remote. We liked that. But it did not give us the solitude we had in the high country. However, it did allow a good view of the distant mountains.

I tried to keep busy. Making pack horse equipment, which I sold, took some of my time. On occasion, I saddled up and helped the ranch and neighbors during weaning and the general fall work of getting cattle ready for the winter.

When Mary and I met friends on the sidewalk of our small western cowtown, they asked if we were going to the cattle sale on Tuesday or the chariot races on Saturday. No one asked if we missed the mountains.

One day in a saddle shop, I met up with one of the hands from the Deer Creek Place. He had recently been on top trying to get winter meat during the late elk season. He told me a disastrous wind had cut a swath down the very draw where our cabin once stood. It left behind uprooted and snapped-off trees. In some places they were piled up two and three high.

"Mark," he said. "That pocket is as much of a tangle of down timber as I've ever seen on the mountain. There is no way a man can ride a horse across that draw now. In fact, it would take somebody like yourself to ever find the place where your cabin stood."

Fall turned into winter. There was a hill where Mary and I went on sunny afternoons. We took our binoculars and looked for white-rumped antelope on the sagebrush flats and along the cutbanks of dry creek beds.

From that same hilltop, we viewed the distant snow-covered mountain ranges. Our eyes followed up the mammoth gash of Powderhorn Canyon to the base of Cougar Mountain. It was home country to us. Mary and I didn't talk much during those times.

As the winter wore on, we found ourselves more often on the hilltop looking at the country that had gripped us and held us for so long. Now that same mountain seemed to hold a gigantic magnet that drew us to it again. Overcome by such a force, we decided to go up to the high country for a visit.

ø ø ø

A few days later found Mary and I pushing one snowshoe ahead of the other up the steep slope of Cougar Mountain. Earlier that morning, a helicopter deposited us on a fairly flat opening lower down. We used the chopper to save time and energy. Now we had the mountain to ourselves as we had known it in the past.

Breaking trail uphill through two to three feet of snow is never easy work. Although our packs were light, we paused often to rest. Mountain chickadees landed on nearby limbs to visit. Red pine squirrels, from higher aloft, scolded loudly, their heads and tails jerking vigorously.

Mary and I continued on up through open forest of mostly Engelmann spruce and Douglas fir. Every step forward was a gain in elevation. The steepness of the slope gave way to a gentle rise. We topped out in a scattered stand of limber pine, stunted and wind-bent. At last, we came out on the edge of a high, rocky rim.

From the lookout point, we gazed upon a vast sweep of high mountain ranges, snow-covered grassland, and deep canyons. It was quiet on the rim. Only the wild cry of a soaring eagle and the sounds of a breeze caressing the needles of limber pine broke the silence of this remote high-up place.

Mary's cheeks were flushed, her eyes bright as she looked around.

"Worth it?" I asked.

"Yes. Very much yes."

The wind of other days had swept most of the snow off the rimrock, and the midday sun had warmed it some. We slipped off our snowshoes and removed the lunch from our packs.

As we munched on sandwiches, we continued to feast our eyes, each in our own way, on the scene before us. Looking far out to the south, our eyes passed over the stark, jagged peaks of the Silver Tips, reaching up toward high-flying cirrus clouds. More to the west, we looked into the wild Tanglefoot Country with its winding streams and treacherous swamps. Closer at hand lay the more gentle, open expanse of

Shonto Park. To the northwest, we could make out the dip in
the skyline that was Agate Creek Divide. We knew beyond
the divide lay the long, beautiful Valley of the Agate.

Our sandwiches finished, Mary and I lingered over hot
tea from our thermos. The one steamy cup was passed back
and forth. Mary said the ritual formed a bond between us,
besides it saved dishes.

Mary and I never stopped looking. Every place our eyes
roamed caused us to recall some adventure we had shared.
Some were wild. Some were tame.

Time passed quickly and the wind freshened. It was
time to get off the rim. Mary and I buckled on snowshoes
and shouldered our packs. We made tracks toward a small
cave we had in mind. There we made camp for the night. It
was a snug place surrounded by low-branched alpine fir and
spruce. Wood for our fire came from snapping off dead
branches that spread above the snow. We melted snow to get
the water we needed.

Supper was simple, and we crawled into sleeping bags
early. Golden stars filled the sky. Beyond the gothic spire of
an alpine fir, I recognized the Gemini twins, Pollux and Cas-
tor, in their proper places.

Mary and I were tired that night, but sleep didn't come
easy. We talked about past years and those to come. We had
come to a fork in the trail. Which branch to take?

I reached out to set more wood on the fire, and we talked
some more. The past twelve years of living in the high country, summer and winter, had given us more fulfillment than
we ever dreamed possible. But now, some events of the recent
past had entered our lives and affected our ability to handle
the lifestyle we had previously chosen. And there weren't just
a couple of factors we had to contend with; there were several. We had a decision to make.

Long ago, Solomon, the man of wisdom, said it well:
To every thing there is a season,
A time for every purpose.
A time to come. A time to go.
The day Mary and I led a string of loaded pack horses up the mountain to start our high country venture was the time to come. Now was the time to go.

The next morning the air was brittle. Sitting on our sleeping bags, we hugged the fire and appreciated our coffee. Mary was adamant about wanting to make a last visit to the site where our cabin had stood.

"I just want to stand out front and look across the canyon to the far peaks one more time," she said.

We hit the trail and started off Cougar Mountain. Our packed trail of the day before made for easy traveling.

At a place where the trail made an abrupt switchback, we stopped on a rocky point. Mary and I squinted against the glare of the winter sun as our eyes followed the sharp backbone of a distant ridge, leading to the low country far away.

That vast basin of foothills and creek-bottom valleys lay under a blanket of silver-white snow. True, it had a different look to it than the mountain we were leaving, but the sheer bigness of it made my heart skip a beat. It was cow country. A country where a man could ride for a long stretch before he had to get off to open a gate.

Here nature's balance was so fragile that wheel tracks made by pioneers' covered wagons still showed in the sod. Along the creeks, Indian artifacts could be found in the loose soil of gopher diggings. It was a country rich in western history, and I never tired of hearing it.

Mary and I continued on down the slope of Cougar Mountain. Below a seep spring, a bull moose nibbled on willows. He lifted his big head and looked our way. With the help of my binoculars, I looked him over, too. I recognized the number on his green ear tag. We knew him well. Moving on, we let him be.

Closer to the place where we had lived, silent-winged gray jays flew from tree to tree, keeping pace with our travel. Mary wondered if they could be some of her friends that ate out of her big spoon when they had visited our camp at dog feeding time.

Then we came to the place where the trail forked. One branch led over a pine-covered ridge into the draw where we had built our cabin years earlier. The other branch led toward the low country far below.

I stopped. Head down, I studied the tip of a snowshoe. I was pulled in two directions by the conflicting thoughts that filled my mind.

Finally, sober-faced and questioning, I turned and met Mary's eyes. Smiling gently, she slowly moved her head from side to side. I turned my head away, giving Mary her moment of privacy.

Then, one behind the other, we made downhill tracks toward the distant big country where a dark blue horizon met a light blue sky.

About the Author

EDWARD MARK McGOUGH was born in 1917 on a New England farm. As a teenager, he left home to sail the seas on a freighter in the European trade. Later, during World War II, he flew in shipbased aircraft in the Atlantic and Pacific theaters.

After the war, McGough attended agricultural college in California where he met and married the girl who became the mother of his three children. Now, the McGoughs are also proud grandparents.

Through the years, McGough has worked on cattle ranches in California, Colorado, and Wyoming. He is quick to declare he considers the twelve years he and his wife spent pioneering "beyond the far ridge" to be a high-point in their lives.

McGough says people find the pronunciation of his last name tricky. When asked how it is properly pronounced, he chuckles and says, "Just remember, it rhymes with cow."

In addition to *Beyond the Far Ridge*, Edward Mark McGough is the author of three young adult westerns.

The cover illustration and illustrations throughout the book are by Victoria Bales.